My Feelings Are Like

Wild Animals!

How Do I Tame Them?

A PRACTICAL GUIDE TO HELP TEENS (AND FORMER TEENS)

FEEL AND DEAL WITH PAINFUL EMOTIONS

Gary Egeberg

PAULIST PRESS

NEW YORK/MAHWAH, N.J.

Dedication

To Wayne Raiter, who walked with me, counseled me, and taught me
during a very painful leg of my journey.
I am forever indebted to you for your compassionate care and wisdom.

Illustrations by H. M. Alan

Cover design by Mark Hicks

Book design by Giorgetta Bell McRee

Library of Congress Cataloging-in-Publication Data

Egeberg, Gary, 1953–
     My feelings are like wild animals! : how do I tame them? / by Gary
Egeberg.
        p. cm.
     Summary: Uses a Christian perspective to explain how to deal with
difficult, unpleasant, or painful emotions such as anger, hate, and
fear.
     ISBN 0-8091-9575-5 (alk. paper)
     1. Teenagers—Religious life. 2. Emotions—Religious aspects—
Christianity—Juvenile literature. [1. Emotions—Religious
aspects—Christianity. 2. Christian life.] I. Title.
BV4531.2.E34   1998
248.8'3—dc21   97-53267
                                                                    CIP
                                                                    AC

Published by Paulist Press
997 Macarthur Boulevard
Mahwah, New Jersey 07430

Printed and bound in the
United States of America

CONTENTS

▲ ▽ ▲ ▽ ▲ ▽ ▲ ▽ ▲ ▽ ▲ ▽ ▲ ▽ ▲ ▽ ▲ ▽ ▲ ▽ ▲ ▽ ▲ ▽ ▲

ACKNOWLEDGEMENTS

▲ ▼ ▲ ▼ ▲ ▼ ▲ ▼ ▲ ▼ ▲ ▼ ▲ ▼ ▲ ▼ ▲ ▼ ▲ ▼ ▲ ▼ ▲ ▼ ▲ ▼ ▲

I would like to thank the many authors I have read over the years who have gifted me with their insights and wisdom. I have learned a lot from all of you. I owe a special thanks to my wife, Peggy, who believed in me and supported me throughout the writing process. Thank you for reading my rough drafts and for your encouragement. I am also grateful to four priests who have been a special blessing in my life: John Clay, Kenneth J. Pierre, Tom Schloemmer, S.J., and Richard E. Pates. I am indebted to my former spiritual director, Virginia Matter, O.S.B., who revealed to me the feminine side of God by her accepting and faithful presence. A special thanks is due to all my junior high students who, over the years, have been my guinea pigs. Your feedback has been instrumental to the unfolding of this book. And finally, I would like to thank Doug Fisher and Karen Scialabba, my editors at Paulist Press, for their many helpful suggestions on how I might more clearly and effectively communicate with you, the reader.

INTRODUCTION

▲ ▼ ▲ ▼ ▲ ▼ ▲ ▼ ▲ ▼ ▲ ▼ ▲ ▼ ▲ ▼ ▲ ▼ ▲ ▼ ▲ ▼ ▲ ▼ ▲

This book is written *for* teens. The teen years can be an exciting and painful time in a person's life. For most teens the years are a mixture of ups and downs. Feeling elated and sad, accepted and rejected, angry and peaceful is part of the emotional terrain teens travel. The image of a mountaintop could represent the "highs," all the fun feelings teens experience, and a dark valley might symbolize the "lows," the unhappy and depressing emotions that teens also encounter in life.

While this book is written primarily for teens, it *can* be used by adults as well. The information and suggested practice skills in this book can help adults express their feelings in healthier ways. Many adults, myself included, were never taught how to handle their difficult and painful emotions. It *is* possible, however, to learn new and better ways of coping with painful emotions no matter what age you are!

But it is for you, the teen, that this book was written. I remember all too well the emotional pain I experienced as a teenager. Unfortunately, I had very few tools to call upon when I felt sad or angry or afraid. Somehow I *survived* these painful feelings, but I sure would have welcomed some <u>information</u> about feelings and some <u>skills</u> to help me express them in constructive ways. I have since acquired some knowledge and skills that I would like to share with you.

Life is not just about survival. When we are hurting emotionally, we not only want to survive the pain but also choose some actions to help us *through* the pain whenever possible. In many cases we don't have to wait for the painful emotions to leave; instead, we can help them along, the way you shoo your younger brother or sister out of your room. Wouldn't you rather feel sad for twenty minutes instead of a couple of hours?! Wouldn't you prefer to feel and deal with your fear in a few minutes rather than suffer for a longer period of time?! Many times, when we activate some tools for coping with our emotions, they will move on more quickly. Not all the time, of course, but more times than not.

It is my hope that this book will be helpful to you as you travel through the teen years and into adulthood. It is my further hope that you will suffer less emotional pain as you encounter the inevitable valleys in life, and enjoy more happy and fulfilling moments as you put into practice some of the suggested skills in each chapter. I wish you the best.

How to Use This Book

▲ ▼ ▲ ▼ ▲ ▼ ▲ ▼ ▲ ▼ ▲ ▼ ▲ ▼ ▲ ▼ ▲ ▼ ▲ ▼ ▲ ▼ ▲

This book does <u>not</u> have to be read from front to back. It would be most helpful, however, if you would take the time to read the first two chapters before reading any of the others. The first two chapters address some general information about feelings that is not covered in the subsequent chapters. For instance, in chapter one you will learn that feelings are neither "good" nor "bad" as we have often thought. Instead, for reasons explored in that chapter, we will label our feelings as either *pleasant* or *unpleasant*. In chapter two you will discover, among other things, that our unpleasant and painful feelings often function as *messengers*, which call us to listen and respond to them.

You might then want to read about a feeling that is particularly challenging or difficult for you, such as anger or fear or shame. Or you might choose to skim through the chapters and read whatever catches your eye.

Chapters three through nine have this format: an introduction, some facts about a particular feeling, followed by some practice skills for coping with that feeling. Throughout each chapter you will find a few interactive writing exercises to which you might consider responding. Most of them do not require too much time. At the end of each chapter is a *Chapter Recap*—a short summary of the chapter's contents for quick reference or review—followed by a few questions to think or write about, or talk over with some friends.

However you choose to interact with this book, do so in a way that fits *your* personality and style. You've already got an <u>A+</u> from me just for looking at the cover!

CHAPTER ONE

▲ ▽ ▲ ▽ ▲ ▽ ▲ ▽ ▲ ▽ ▲ ▽ ▲ ▽ ▲ ▽ ▲ ▽ ▲ ▽ ▲ ▽ ▲ ▽ ▲

Naming and Taming Our Feelings: Getting Started

INTRODUCTION

Have you ever smashed something in anger or slammed a door or hurled something you treasured against a wall? Have you ever felt *so* angry that you lost *all* control of what came out of your mouth—perhaps you yelled, screamed, and swore? Or have you ever felt deeply afraid about something or of someone but were unable to talk about your fear? Did you ever say or do something that left you feeling weighed down by a ton of guilt and had no idea how to get out from under this heavy load? Has the thought of suicide ever entered your mind when things seemed to be going totally wrong?

If you answered yes to any or all of the above, you are *not* alone. Many teens—and many adults for that matter—can answer yes to some or all of these questions. I could answer yes to **ALL** of them during my adolescence. When I was a teen, I experienced powerful and painful feelings and didn't have the skills for coping with them constructively. As an adult, I have gained many skills to help me feel and deal with my emotions. You can learn and practice healthy habits for handling your emotions *right now* while you are a teen! You don't have to wait for adulthood. In fact, as a young person, you may end up possessing more tools to express your emotions than many adults!

As the title of this book suggests, feelings *can* be like wild animals at times. Before a wild horse can be safely ridden, it must be tamed. Our feelings, especially our strongest ones, also need to be tamed. When we control our feelings—rather than allow them to control us—we can "ride" through life more safely and enjoyably. As young people move toward maturity and adulthood, one of their challenges is to harness their feelings a bit, so that they are not hurting themselves and others as much as when their feelings are left to run wild. This is not an easy task (and you won't do it perfectly), but you *will* experience many benefits now and throughout your life as you gain the ability to express your feelings in positive ways.

YOU WILL BE PAID FOR LEARNING!

You will be paid for improving your ability to express your feelings constructively and healthily. How? First, you will receive the huge paycheck of feeling better about yourself. Isn't feeling good about ourselves worth at least a million dollars? Would you and I want a million dollars *if* we could only have it in exchange for our happiness? Secondly, you will enjoy better relationships with friends, classmates, peers, coaches, teachers, parents . . . and yourself, *if* you are willing to learn and practice some new ways to cope with your feelings. A third payoff will be your capacity to activate some simple and practical tools to *help yourself right now* when you are in emotional pain. Whether you are feeling the pain of loneliness or rejection, anger or rage, fear or hate, you will be able to choose some practice skills from this book to help yourself through and beyond these powerful emotions. Your feelings won't have to control you; instead, you will learn some ways to control them.

SQUIRRELS AND ANGER

Just for fun match each feeling below with the animal that might best fit it. There are no right or wrong answers, but if you match the feeling of anger with a squirrel, be prepared to defend your choice.

M	fear	A.	bear
H	anger	B.	hound dog
E	loneliness	C.	dove
D	shyness	D.	deer
N	peacefulness	E.	elephant
F	jealousy	F.	squirrel
A	guilt	G.	wolverine
I	boredom	H.	bull
B	nervousness	I.	turtle
G	hatred	J.	hyena
K	happiness	K	sheep
L	sadness	L.	snake
J	rage	M.	coyote
C	love	N.	otter
O	excitement	O.	lion

2

Perhaps you were able to somewhat logically match up ten or more of the feelings with an appropriate animal. Maybe when you got to the last five or so you had to stretch a bit in order to find a good match, or perhaps you filled the remaining blanks with any leftover letter because of limited choices. If you could have chosen other animals to pair up with those last five feelings, you might have been able to complete the entire "assignment" in a more logical way. And if you were to compare your "answers" with a classmate's or friend's, a healthy debate might develop over whose choices were more reasonable and "right."

TAKE ME TO YOUR LEADER: INTELLIGENCE

One reason for doing the previous matching exercise is to demonstrate how we try to approach things logically and intelligently. Logic and intelligence helped us match some feelings and animals in a reasonable and sensible manner. So, too, our intelligence is going to be a key player in expressing our emotions in healthy and constructive ways. **Our mind, our intelligence, is the part of our humanness we want to put in charge of our feelings**. This, of course, is <u>not</u> always easy to do. Sometimes our feelings run off, leaving our minds far behind, especially when we're upset.

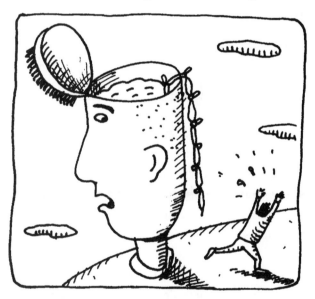

When we are emotionally upset and do something impulsive, we call it **reacting**. If we could do over again what our feelings have sometimes led us to do, if we could **re-act** it, we would often choose different and more intelligent behavior. Usually when you and I react emotionally, without much use of our intelligence, we have a consequence of some sort to pay. When I angrily blurt out something, I usually end up hurting another person by my *thought-less* words and hurt myself with the consequence of guilt. If I could have taken some time to let my anger cool down, which my *intelligence* can invite and *lead* me to do, then I might not have hurt someone with my words and I wouldn't be suffering the pain of guilt.

Think of your intelligence as being like a responsible babysitter who takes very good care of a small child while her parents are out for dinner. A good babysitter would make sure the child stays safe and would <u>not</u> allow the child to do anything that would endanger herself. In this analogy the teen babysitter would represent our intelligence and the child would symbolize our emotions. We want the babysitter (our intelligence) to be in charge of the small child (our emotions) and not the other way around.

The use of our intelligence is going to be our leader in expressing our feelings healthily. This does not mean we are going to become emotionless robots. Our feelings are a wonderful part of being human! Our feelings *and* our mind can be very good friends and need to work together in our lives.

They can and should be partners, but usually we want our intelligence to lead our good friend and partner, feelings.

FEELINGS: EITHER PLEASANT OR UNPLEASANT

Many of us have come to believe that some feelings such as joy, love, peace, and happiness are good, and some feelings such as anger, jealousy, and hatred are bad. We are going to toss this belief about feelings out the window! Sometimes to learn new things we have to do some unlearning! Let's unlearn and relearn.

When we label certain emotions as "bad," we are starting off on the wrong foot toward emotional health. Feelings are neither good nor bad in the same way that sharing with someone is "good" and stealing from someone is "bad." Instead, feelings simply inform us of what's going on inside of us and are an important part of being human. We have a very wide range of emotions and can feel them at different levels of intensity, from very mild to very strong. Anger, a so-called "bad" emotion, can have a "good" purpose for being in our lives, which we will learn about in the chapter on anger. For now, let's begin to let go of the habit of labeling feelings as "good" or "bad."

One major reason we even have feelings is to bring us information or messages. For example, jealousy can tell me that I'm not feeling very good about myself and my sinking self-esteem may need a boost. Hate may bring me the message that I have something to work out with another person. Loneliness may make me aware of my need for friends. Joy could be telling me that I am proud of a goal I achieved. Peace may bring me the message that my life is in balance and things are going pretty well. From these examples, we can see that all our emotions—even the ones we used to think were "bad"—can bring important messages to our awareness.

Because emotions are part of our state of consciousness (what's going on inside us), and have important messages to share with us, we will no longer call some of them "good" and some of them "bad." Let's retrain ourselves to label them as either **pleasant** or **unpleasant**. Some emotions are obviously very unpleasant to *feel*, but that doesn't make them bad. (Most of us would rather feel the pleasant feeling of happiness instead of the unpleasant feeling of sadness.) What tends to be good or bad about our feelings is how we choose to *express* them. If in our anger we hit someone, we have chosen "bad" or poor behavior. Or, in the midst of our anger, if we take some time to cool off, we have chosen "good" or constructive behavior.

Make a list of emotions that are most frequently considered to be either pleasant or unpleasant (the ones we used to call good or bad). I'll start you off. See if you can add ten or twenty or more to each group.

Pleasant Feelings
peacefulness, joy, acceptance

_____

_____

_____

_____

Unpleasant Feelings
fear, anger, rejection

_____

_____

_____

_____

FROM UNPLEASANT TO PLEASANT FEELINGS: THE PURPOSE OF THIS BOOK

When you looked at the table of contents, you might have thought, "This book is really going to be depressing—all those painful feelings!" You may have wondered if you are going to feel better or *worse* after reading it! My experience is that when we *deal with* our unpleasant and painful emotions, we have a better chance of enjoying the pleasant ones. When we cope with our fear, we regain calm and trust and confidence. When we deal with our shame and guilt, we experience the priceless gift of inner peace and feel better about ourselves. When we forgive someone, we enjoy a restored and renewed relationship. So it is my hope that this book will help you (and me) through the painful and unpleasant feelings, so that you (and I) can once again enjoy the pleasant feelings. We *must* face and deal with our unpleasant and painful emotions if we want to feel good again!

Our emotions are a gift to us from God. During the teen years they tend to be a challenging gift to handle—like an untamed horse—because of the intensity of a young person's feelings and because of how quickly they change. You may have awakened one morning feeling quite crabby and then felt happiness when you saw your friends at school. As the day progressed, you may have experienced anger and hurt when someone teased you too much, joy at getting a good grade on a test, and embarrassed when you dropped your books! That's a lot to feel in one day, and you haven't even gotten home from school yet to discover your younger brother or sister in *your* room messing with *your* stuff—not to mention how upset Mom is going to get with you because you forgot to take out the garbage and said something hurtful to your kid brother or sister!

Because the emotions young people feel are so intense and change very rapidly, some skills are needed to handle these powerful God-given gifts. If we are upset and let our emotions run wild, we are lacking the health and wholeness our God desires for us. On the other hand, if we don't allow ourselves to feel anything (this is a problem some adults tend to have more than teens), we are also lacking health and wholeness.

Another image for wild, uncontrolled feelings might be a zoo in which the animals are on the loose and out of control. Without any ways to protect the visitors from the roaming animals, such a zoo would be a dangerous place to visit. When our feelings, like the zoo animals, are allowed to "roam" without any restrictions, the potential for chaos and destruction is much greater than when we put some restraints on them.

THREE TOOLS TO HELP US ON OUR JOURNEY TOWARD EMOTIONAL HEALTH AND WHOLENESS

Imagine that you have just been told you are going all by yourself to a foreign country tomorrow and you don't know the language or the customs of the people! How would you communicate your basic needs? Perhaps you could point to your stomach to indicate your hunger or pretend you are drinking a glass of water to show your hosts you are thirsty. But how would you communicate your fear or sadness or excitement? How could you communicate your desire to go home?

If, however, you had a year to prepare for this trip to a foreign country, you would obviously work hard to learn its language and customs, and as you learned the language, you would want to practice it as much as possible. Furthermore, because such a trip would excite and scare you a little, you might choose to spend some time praying for strength and courage. These three tools for our fantasy—or nightmare!—trip are also the three basic tools we need when it comes to "traveling" into the land of unpleasant feelings:
* **Knowledge** * **Practice skills** * **Involving God**

Our First Tool: KNOWLEDGE

Before we journey deeper into the foreign and familiar "country" of feelings, let's learn something about them. Somehow, we have come to believe some wrong messages and "information" about emotions. For instance, boys sometimes pick up the message that they shouldn't cry or show sensitivity because it means they are weak or not "tough." Girls frequently have learned that getting angry is less acceptable for them than it is for boys. "Nice" girls don't get angry. Both sexes have picked up some inaccurate information about feelings and/or information that just isn't very helpful. These inaccuracies that you may have learned have not been intentionally passed on to you by your parents or teachers or others in our society. No one has purposely misled you. The fact is that as a society we are just beginning to learn the truth about feelings and how to handle them in healthy ways. You belong to one of the first generations to be able to learn this "new" information and practice it in your lives—especially at such a young age!   As I mentioned earlier, I learned a lot of what I am sharing with you when I became an adult. You don't have to wait that long. In fact, you can begin today!

Before we look at some examples of new and more helpful information about feelings, take a minute or two and write down in the spaces below what you have learned about these feelings:

*Here is what I have learned about **fear** in my life so far:* _____

_____

_____

_____

*Here is what I have learned about **hate** in my life so far:* _____

_____

_____

_____

*Here is what I have learned about **shame and guilt** in my life so far:* _____

_____

_____

_____

I'm willing to wager that you wrote down some very good insights about these unpleasant feelings. And I wouldn't be surprised if you, like me, had some inaccuracies about these feelings as well. Now take a look at what we are beginning to learn about these emotions.

FEAR. Did you know that the "ear" in the word "f<u>ear</u>" is a reminder to listen to fear's messages for us? Did you know that healthy fear needs to be listened to—even though it is unpleasant to feel—because it wants to help us stay safe? Unhealthy fear, on the other hand, wants to bully us and keep us from taking any risks in life and needs to be confronted. Do you know how to tell the difference between healthy and unhealthy fear?

HATE. Are you aware that the "ate" in the word "h<u>ate</u>" lets us know that the hate we sometimes feel toward someone will continue "eating" away at us until we deal with it? Have you ever learned about the six stages we must pass through to get beyond our hate, the first of which is to give ourselves *permission* to <u>feel hate</u> toward someone rather than trying to stop or stuff it?

SHAME AND GUILT. Did you know that the "am" in the word "sh<u>am</u>e" tries to tell us we are *bad* when we make a poor choice ("I <u>AM</u> BAD!") and that this is a lie that only makes us feel worse and more powerless to take any positive action? And that the "ui" in the word "g<u>ui</u>lt" tells me that you (u) have been hurt by something I (i) did, and I need to take some corrective action that will help you and me feel better? Or did you know we can be feeling a combination of both shame and guilt, and that there are some specific steps you and I can take to move beyond these painful and unpleasant emotions?

These are just a few examples of the knowledge about feelings we will explore in this book. Knowledge *about* something is important but <u>not</u> enough. After we have some knowledge, we need to call on another tool.

Our Second Tool: PRACTICE SKILLS

You and I can have knowledge about how a bicycle works, but until we get on the bike and try to ride it, our knowledge is not worth very much. Should our bike break down somewhere, then our knowledge can help us fix it. The same is true with feelings. We can have a lot of knowledge *about* feelings, but until we apply and *practice* our knowledge in real-life situations with real people, it won't help us very much.

Let's look at the same feelings we did on the previous page. This time write down how you usually *handle these feelings (whether constructively and positively or not), then write down some healthy ways people your age could cope with them.*

*Here's how I usually cope with **fear:** _____*

_____

_____

_____

Some other positive ways teens could cope with feeling fear are _____

_____

_____

_____

*Here's how I usually cope with feeling **hate:** _____*

_____

_____

_____

Some other positive ways teens could cope with feeling hate are _____

_____

_____

_____

*Here's how I usually cope with **shame and guilt**: _____*

_____

_____

_____

Some other positive ways teens could cope with feeling shame and guilt are _____

_____

_____

_____

Now compare your insights and wisdom with what follows:

FEAR. One way to reduce our fears is to breathe properly for a few minutes, which will enable that sinking, fluttery feeling in our stomach to settle down a bit. Another fear-coping skill is to write down what we are afraid of in great detail and then analyze what we have written to see if our fears are at all rational or reasonable. If our fears aren't rational, we can then choose to kick them out and redirect our attention elsewhere.

HATE. A very effective way to deal with the hate we are feeling is to write a letter to the person we are hating. In this letter we would hold nothing back! We would then rip up the letter and throw it away. This simple action helps to lessen the intensity of our hate as we pour it out of our hearts and minds and onto the paper. Another way to cope with hate is to remember that it takes time to heal and we needn't feel bad when we are stuck in hate.

SHAME AND GUILT. A great way to get free from shame's crippling grip is to make a list of all of our good qualities and the good things we have done, and then read it often. The more we do this, the more we see that we are indeed a GOOD PERSON and not the bad person shame would have us believe. A simple but challenging way to lessen our feelings of guilt is to make amends with the person we have harmed.

These are just a few samples of the many, many skills you will find in this book to help you cope with and express your feelings in healthy and constructive ways. You and I can have all the *knowledge* in the world about feelings and have a wide variety of *practice skills* to choose from, but because we are imperfect people we are still going to blow it at times. We will never express our feelings perfectly. We will still hurt others and ourselves from time to time. Fortunately, we have a loving God to forgive us and assist us when we fail to express our emotions healthily. I still blow it at times and seek God's forgiveness so that I can try again. I hope you, too, will turn to God for forgiveness and strength to begin again when you blow it.

Our Third Tool: INVOLVING GOD

You might be wondering why God is listed as our third tool rather than our first. Of course God *is* first in that God is The Giver of our all our gifts: our feelings, our mind, and the ability to learn new skills. But a prayer such as "help me deal with my anger" is answered, in part, by learning and practicing new skills. These three tools are like the sides of a triangle. Each side is crucial to the other two sides in learning to express our emotions in healthy and constructive ways. There will be a time to focus on one side of the triangle more than the other two, depending on what we need. There will be a time to learn, a time to practice, and a time to pray.

God has at least five very special gifts to offer us as we practice, fail, learn, and grow in our emotional life. God invites us to open as widely as possible to these much-needed gifts.

God offers us the gift of unconditional love. In other words, no matter how poorly we express our feelings, we are loved continuously by our God. We don't earn God's love by having success with our feelings. God just simply and *always* loves us! This love is so important to us when we experience the ups and downs of our emotions.

God offers us the gift of consolation and comfort. Despite having knowledge and some success with our feelings, we will still forget and/or fail to put into practice what we know at times and feel badly about it. We have a God who is more like a gentle mother than a mean judge who will come to us at times like these and wrap us in love and be with us in our pain. God's mothering love consoles us so that we can feel nurtured enough to try again.

God offers the gift of companionship and friendship. God is a friend who is always available to us, and we can pray any time we want. God is a faithful friend who will stick with us during the ups and downs of our emotional life.

God offers the gift of acceptance. Again, when we blow it, when we screw up, God doesn't reject us; rather, God accepts us *completely*. We may reject ourselves and others may reject us, but God *always* accepts us, even when our behavior has been at its worst.

God offers us the gift of forgiveness. When you and I fail, God simply says, "Okay, what can you learn from this?" And God delights in us when we are able to learn from our mistakes and make progress in handling our feelings with increasing maturity and wisdom.

Do you see why it makes sense to have the Giver of Gifts on your team? These wonderful gifts from our loving God are yours if you want to accept them: unconditional love, consolation and comfort, companionship and friendship, acceptance, and forgiveness!

CHAPTER RECAP

1) Three payoffs for learning how to express your emotions in healthy ways are:
   a) you will feel better about yourself;
   b) you will have better relationships with friends, peers, classmates, adults, and yourself;
   c) you will be able to help yourself when you are hurting emotionally.

2) Generally speaking, our intelligence (our minds) should lead our feelings rather than the other way around—especially when we are upset.

3) We can label feelings as either *pleasant* or *unpleasant* instead of referring to some of them as "good" and some of them as "bad."

4) This book is meant to help you move through and beyond your unpleasant and painful feelings so that you can once again enjoy the pleasant and less painful ones.

5) Emotions, in their wildest and most untamed state, can sometimes hurt us and/or others. We need to learn how to tame them a bit.

6) We have three major tools to help us grow into emotional health and wholeness: accurate knowledge, practice skills that must be practiced, and our teammate and supporter, God.

For Reflection, Journaling, or Discussion

1) Which three feelings are most unpleasant or difficult for you? Can you think of a few times recently when you experienced these feelings? _____

_____

_____

_____

_____

2) What are the two or three most important or helpful facts you learned about feelings in this chapter?

_____

_____

_____

_____

3) If I chose to share something from this chapter with my parent(s), it would be: _____

_____

_____

_____

_____

With a friend I might share: _____

_____

_____

_____

_____

CHAPTER TWO

▲ ▼ ▲ ▽ ▲ ▽ ▲ ▽ ▲ ▽ ▲ ▽ ▲ ▽ ▲ ▽ ▲ ▽ ▲ ▽ ▲ ▽ ▲ ▽ ▲ ▼ ▲

Pleasant Facts about Unpleasant Feelings

INTRODUCTION

Running sprints up and down a gym floor is <u>not</u> most basketball players' idea of fun, but they huff and puff through these drills in order to have the necessary endurance to compete in a game. Lifting weights, which many young athletes do, is not particularly enjoyable, but athletes grunt and groan and strain their muscles to be strong enough for their sport. All sports involve *some* unpleasant drills as part of the necessary training and preparation for the games, matches, and contests to come. Most junior high and high school students do not rejoice when their coaches put them through these drills, but they cooperate because they know it will make them better athletes. The *unpleasant* and sometimes painful drills are accepted as part of participating in sports. Without the drills, young athletes would be less successful against the competition they face.

Unpleasant and painful emotions are like these drills and routines a coach might put you through; the pleasant feelings are like the game or contest itself. Just as the drills have a positive benefit, unpleasant emotions have a positive side to them as well. When we deal with our unpleasant feelings, we can play more effectively in the "game of life"—the most wonderful game of all! Let's look at some positive—if not "pleasant"—facts about these emotions. None of us likes *feeling* these unpleasant emotions, but they are as much a part of life as drills are a part of sports.

12

TEN BASIC FACTS ABOUT UNPLEASANT OR PAINFUL EMOTIONS

1) Unpleasant feelings contribute to the quality and meaning of our lives. The fact that we can feel so many different emotions at all different levels of intensity adds so much to life! We have the capacity as human beings to feel happy or sad, secure or insecure, angry or calm . . . and we are richer because of it. Without the diversity of our emotional life, we would be more like perfect—*perfectly boring*—robots than people. Even though you and I don't like pain at all, most of us would rather have the capacity to feel both pleasant *and* unpleasant emotions rather than just the pleasant ones <u>all</u> the time. We all want our personal lives and our world to be better, but a perfect world of continuous happiness does not appeal to most of us. Like the change of seasons, we appreciate the ability to feel different emotions. The wider range and variety of feelings we can experience, the richer our lives are, and *part* of that range and variety includes the unpleasant and painful emotions.

2) Unpleasant feelings bring us information. When we get sick, our bodies tell us that something is physically wrong. When we experience unpleasant emotions, our feelings tell us that something is hurting inside us that may need some attention. When we feel lonely, loneliness *tells us* we need the company of a caring friend or relative. When we feel fear, fear *tells us* to be careful or to stop what we are doing. When we feel hate, hate may be *telling us* that we are unhappy with ourselves or that we need to work out a problem with the person we are hating. Our unpleasant feelings bring us information that we need to listen to.

3) Unpleasant feelings often want a response from us. Have you ever had the frustration of sharing something really important with a friend or parent and you knew by their response—or lack of response—that they didn't *really* hear you?! You shared something that really excited or troubled you and they didn't seem to listen closely or appreciate how important it was to you! You wanted a *response* from your listener but got none. Unpleasant feelings also want a response from us. Like you, they want to be listened to and taken seriously.

First, they want us to recognize they are there. We can recognize our feelings simply by *acknowledging them*, by <u>naming what we are feeling</u>. This naming of our feelings is the first step toward making a healthy choice about what to do with the feelings. By saying what we are feeling to ourselves mentally or whispering it aloud, we are acknowledging our feelings. At any given time of the day— and *especially* when we are in emotional pain—we can simply name the feeling we are experiencing. "Right now I feel sad. . . . " "I feel angry. . . . " "I'm really feeling lonely these days. . . . " This is a way of recognizing our feelings, a way of saying I *really* hear you.

13

Secondly, our unpleasant feelings want us to treat them with honor and respect. One of the greatest ways to show honor and respect to another person is to listen to them and take them seriously. The same is true of our feelings. We show our feelings honor and respect by *listening to them and taking them seriously.* We can do this by naming them and by listening carefully to what they may be trying to tell us.

EXAMPLES: I feel sad right now (naming) and I am not going to ignore this sadness (taking them seriously).
I feel angry (naming) and I'm not going to stuff my angry feelings (taking them seriously).

Thirdly, our unpleasant and painful feelings want us to choose a course of action that will lessen their intensity whenever we can. The two we mentioned above, naming and showing respect, are good beginnings, but often more is needed. When you are hurting, you may need a friend or parent to do *more* than listen to you and take you seriously. You might need the *caring actions* of a hug or a phone call or a card that shows how important you are to them. Our unpleasant feelings also need more from us at times. Our unpleasant and painful emotions often want and need *self-caring action* from us. If we are feeling lonely, this feeling would appreciate it if we would try to connect with someone. If we're feeling sad, sadness would want us to do some reflecting about what might be causing this sadness and determine if there are some simple steps we can take to lessen the sadness.

What are some self-caring actions you can take when you are hurting emotionally? _____

_____

_____

_____

4) Feelings are changing rather than permanent; both pleasant *and* unpleasant feelings come and go like visitors. This is a very difficult fact to remember about feelings—*especially* when we are hurting. Sometimes when we feel down or depressed, we don't think our feelings are *ever* going to change, but they will! *These painful feelings will pass.* Or if we are really feeling good one day, we can know that this feeling will go on its way too and be replaced by another feeling. A visual to help us remember this might be boats on the sea or fish in the sea. The current of life brings all sorts of feelings into us and carries them on their way out of us. Our challenge is to flow with all of our feelings—especially with our painful feelings—confident that we *will* feel better again.

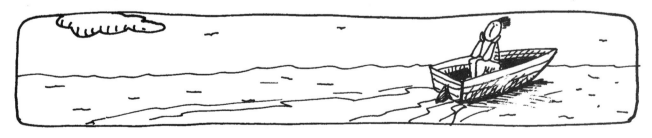

5) There is a cycle to feelings, just as there is a cycle to nature. We experience ups and downs, pleasant and unpleasant feelings in our emotional life. We need to get to know this cycle and remember it—especially when we are at the bottom of the cycle. *Our feelings will cycle up again.* When we are experiencing our most painful emotions, when we are at the bottom of this cycle, *we believe that our pain will pass*, this unpleasant and painful emotional state *will* move out of us and a more pleasant and less painful emotional state will move in. Of course, when we are really hurting, it NEVER seems like the pain will leave, it NEVER seems like we will experience happiness again, BUT WE WILL!!!!

 Nature serves as a great model for this up-and-down cycle. In the midst of a long and cold winter, spring doesn't seem like it will ever come, but it ALWAYS does. The winter pain of our unpleasant and painful feelings will give way to the spring of pleasant and less painful emotions. Spring brings new life, and we enjoy new life as well when our unpleasant and painful feelings pass.

6) We cannot (in most cases) *instantly* get rid of our unpleasant feelings, but we *CAN* (in most cases) take some steps to help ourselves when we are experiencing painful emotions. When we are feeling sadness or fear or anger or any unpleasant emotion, we can usually take *some* steps to lessen the intensity of our pain. We can participate in our own healing. When you take a remedy for a sore throat, you participate in your healing by taking the medication as directed and by getting rest. When we are hurting emotionally, we can often take two very important steps to help ourselves so that we don't hurt as much or for as long as we would if we took no action.

First, we make a conscious decision not to engage in any self-destructive action. For some of us, our painful feelings hurt so badly that our pain blinds us from seeing ways in which we can help ourselves. We may even blame *ourselves* for our pain and experience a self-destructive desire to punish ourselves! We feel like we have to take *some* action in response to our pain (we can't just sit there in such deep pain!), and sometimes drinking, using drugs, letting schoolwork slide, and acting out with other destructive behaviors—even thoughts of or attempts at suicide—may seem like the only options we have. But we choose to <u>not</u> give into these unhealthy and destructive ways of responding to our pain! When we choose not to *self-destruct*, we then need to make a choice to *self-construct*, to take some action that will help us through and beyond the pain. Avoiding self-destructive behaviors is a crucial beginning that we can be very proud of, but it calls for another step.

Second, we can remind ourselves that we have some positive, healthy, and constructive options from which to choose. Choices give us a sense of personal power, and the more positive choices we have, the more likely it is we will choose wisely and well. For example, we can make a list of choices we have when we are hurting. Here's an example of how Carlos, a sixteen-year-old sophomore, helps himself self-construct:

"Carlos feels depressed. He is going to show respect and honor to this feeling by taking it seriously. He chooses to make a list of simple actions he can take to help lift himself out of this depression into a less depressed state":

> I can call Juanita or Nate and see if either of them wants to do something.
> I can write in my journal.
> I can go for a walk.
> I can talk to my parent(s) or another trusted adult.
> I can do something I enjoy like shooting baskets.

• • •

By generating this list, Carlos has come up with a menu of sorts from which he can choose some simple action or actions to help himself. He might still feel depressed after doing one or more of these, but he *increases his chances* of feeling a little better. When we take some action, we may change our mood completely!

Pretend you are John in the following scenario. A fifteen-year-old ninth grader, John is very upset because his parents just had a huge fight again. They were talking about divorce, which depresses him so much that he finds himself having dark and destructive thoughts. Make a list (a menu) of constructive choices that John could choose from to help himself through this difficult time.

1) _____   2) _____

3) _____   4) _____

5) _____   6) _____

7) _____   8) _____

7) **Feelings—especially unpleasant feelings—seek expression; they seek to be released so that they can leave us.** Feelings, as we mentioned previously, never want to set up a permanent home in us. By their nature they want to move on. If we don't express them, if we don't release them, they can become stuck in us. Unpleasant emotions can make us ill—physically, emotionally, mentally, and spiritually. If we never express our anger, it stays stuck in us. If we don't express our fears, we pay the price of not taking the risks we need to take in order to experience greater satisfaction in life. If we don't express our sadness, we suffer longer than we need to. So to avoid getting sick, *we must express our unpleasant feelings.* Generally speaking, there are two ways we can express our feelings:

in a positive manner	or	in a negative manner
in a healthy way	or	an unhealthy way
with constructive behavior	or	with destructive behavior
in a mature style	or	an immature style
in a life-giving form	or	a life-diminishing form

We will explore many skills in the chapters to follow with which to practice healthy and positive emotional expression. For now, the important thing to remember is that unpleasant and painful emotions *want* to be released, which happens best when we consciously choose to express them in constructive ways.

8) We are responsible for our feelings and for how we choose to express them. So many people of all ages play the "blame game." I learned to play this game very well, but I always lost when I played it, even though I was a very good "blamer." Eventually I learned it's a worthless game because it has <u>no</u> winners. Blaming <u>never</u> solves anything. We may be used to saying "*you* make me so mad" or "*you* ruined my day," which isn't true, and even if it were true, it wouldn't make us *feel* any better. We again toss this old and unhealthy way of interacting out the window and replace it with a conscious choice to be responsible for our own feelings and for how we choose to express them. One way to do this is to state how we feel *about* someone's behavior. This does not place blame; instead, it informs in behavioral terms what the person can work toward changing if he or she chooses.

"I statement" about our feelings		other person's behavior
I feel angry	when	you say you're going to call me but then you don't.
I feel sad	when	you put me down.
I feel afraid	when	you and Dad fight so much.

Add five more examples of "I" statements about someone's behavior. You can use real situations and people or fictitious ones.

1) I feel _____ *when* _____

2) I feel _____ *when* _____

3) I feel _____ *when* _____

4) I feel _____ *when* _____

5) I feel _____ *when* _____

9) Our thoughts produce our feelings rather than the other way around. Psychologists tell us that *how we think* about an event determines *how we feel*. Here is an example of how two eighth graders, Jenny and Amy, think about the same events in their lives and the different feelings that result from their thinking:

Event: Someone gossips about Jenny.
Thought: She thinks they shouldn't do that and she "can't" stop thinking about it.
Feeling: She feels very hurt and upset.

Event: Someone gossips about Amy.
Thought: Amy thinks, "I'm not going to let it bother me. It's not true."
Feeling: Very little upset feeling

In the example above, the way the person thought about the event led to the subsequent feelings she had. The way each of us thinks about the things that happen to us in life very much influences the emotions we will experience.

10) We might need to seek professional help in dealing with our unpleasant emotions. We are so fortunate to live in a time when there are good counselors and other professionals to whom we can turn for help with our emotional pain! I very much needed to see a counselor during my life and have been helped a lot. I have no shame or embarrassment about this. In fact, if there were a bumper sticker that said, "I HAVE BEEN HELPED BY MY COUNSELOR!" I might very well put it on my car. If you or I broke an arm, we wouldn't call a plumber. When we are having a lot of problems in life, which usually means we are also having a lot of emotional pain, we wouldn't go see a car mechanic. This is just common sense. So please do not think this or any book can be a substitute for receiving professional counseling if you need it. If the emotions you are experiencing are very extreme and leading you to act or consider acting in destructive ways, please seek professional help! Especially if you are feeling suicidal, you need to get help NOW! Pick up the phone and dial 911 and the operator can hook you up with someone who can help you. Also, there is an appendix of emergency numbers in the back of this book on page 89 which can help you locate some immediate help. Don't be afraid to use it. Remember, YOU ARE IMPORTANT TO GOD AND OTHER PEOPLE AND WORTHY OF GETTING THE HELP YOU NEED! PEOPLE CAN ONLY HELP YOU, HOWEVER, IF *YOU* REACH OUT!

We have identified ten crucial understandings we need to have as we journey into the land of unpleasant feelings. We will revisit these ten key facts frequently in the chapters to come, as well as add to these.

CHAPTER RECAP

Ten important facts about feelings are:

1) Unpleasant feelings add to the quality and meaning of our lives.

2) Unpleasant feelings bring us information.

3) Unpleasant feelings often want a response from us: recognition, respect, and some action to lessen their intensity.

4) Feelings are changing rather than permanent. Pleasant and unpleasant emotions come and go.

5) There is an up-and-down cycle to feelings. When we are at the bottom, our challenge is to remember that we will cycle up again.

6) We cannot usually get rid of our unpleasant feelings instantly. We can, however, take some simple actions to help ourselves through the pain.

7) Feelings—especially unpleasant feelings—seek expression and release.

8) We are responsible for our feelings and for how we choose to express them.

9) How we think about an event or about what happens to us determines how we feel.

10) We may need to seek professional counseling for help with our painful emotions.

For Reflection, Journaling, or Discussion

1) Do you agree that being able to feel unpleasant and painful emotions adds to the richness of life? Why or why not? _____

_____

_____

_____

Would you rather have a world in which we could feel no pain? _____ *Explain.* _____

_____

_____

_____

_____

2) What are three fairly common self-destructive or unhealthy ways with which many teenagers try to cope with their painful emotions? Why do you think some teens choose these destructive ways?

_____

_____

_____

_____

What are three self-constructive or healthy ways that you have seen teens—including yourself—express their unpleasant and painful feelings? _____

_____

_____

_____

_____

3) Interview a parent or other adult about his/her most painful feelings as a teenager and how he/she dealt with these feelings. Person interviewed: _____

Most painful feelings were: _____

_____

How he/she dealt with these feelings: _____

_____

_____

_____

_____

CHAPTER THREE

▲ ▽ ▲ ▽ ▲ ▽ ▲ ▽ ▲ ▽ ▲ ▽ ▲ ▽ ▲ ▽ ▲ ▽ ▲ ▽ ▲ ▽ ▲ ▽ ▲ ▽ ▲

Anger: What Should I Do With It?

INTRODUCTION

ANGER is a feeling that many of us struggle with—especially if we are trying to live as Christians. Because we try to follow Jesus' Way of Life, perhaps we think that we should *never* feel anger or that we are "bad" people or "bad" Christians when we do experience angry feelings. Because this emotion is one that almost everyone has at least some difficulty with—whether it is the difficulty of expressing it appropriately or the challenge of receiving another person's anger—we have our work cut out for us in learning how to handle it better.

This is probably a good time to remind you (and me) that we are *not* going to deal perfectly with any of our unpleasant feelings—especially not one as challenging and difficult as anger. We will make progress and we will backslide. We will express our anger in really healthy ways at times, and at other times we will revert to unhealthy or destructive ways. So please do not expect to read this chapter and think that you have your anger "problem" (challenge) licked. There are millions of teens and millions of adults who have struggled with and continue to struggle with this emotion, so you and I have lots of company in our struggle with anger.

You may know people at one extreme of the continuum who *never* express their anger; nothing *seems* to ever upset them! At the other end you may know some people who express their anger in unhealthy and inappropriate ways; everything seems to upset them! While we might be tempted to admire the people who seemingly never get angry, they are lacking health and wholeness as much as the people who "blow up" when they feel angry. To not own or express our anger is more acceptable in our society, but it is not the path to health and wholeness Jesus calls us to. *Jesus felt and dealt with his anger*, and if we truly want to follow his Way of Life (which we all know is not easy), we too must deal with our anger. We need to aim for that vast middle ground in between the extremes of stuffing our anger and of expressing our anger in an unhealthy way.

THE OLD UNHEALTHY WAYS OF EXPRESSING OUR ANGER

Slamming doors, throwing things, screaming, yelling, swearing, insulting, hitting, hurting, taking it out on someone, silent treatment, crying, stuffing it, ignoring or avoiding someone, getting even. . . . Does any of this sound familiar? It does to me and probably to at least half of the world! I even *mastered* some of the unhealthy ways mentioned above. And I wouldn't be surprised if you are on your way to mastering some of these ways of expressing your anger as well. With lots of hard work, patience, and forgiveness for the times I have failed, these old ways are no longer my main methods for handling my anger. Yes, occasionally I do revert to an old way, but I usually recognize it quickly, make amends, and choose a healthier method of expressing my anger. I am *not* a master of healthy anger expression, but I am a student who is learning better ways of coping with anger, and I invite you to be a fellow student, a fellow learner. Because you are so young, as you practice healthier ways of expressing your anger, you may indeed, some day, become a master of healthy anger expression.

Of the old, unhealthy ways of expressing anger mentioned above, which one or ones do you sometimes use to express your anger? _____

_____

_____

_____

_____

_____

ANGER IS ABOUT HURT

According to the dictionary, anger is defined as "a strong feeling of displeasure and belligerence aroused by a real or supposed wrong." The key word is *WRONG*. When we feel anger it is because we have been wronged or *felt* we have been wronged by another person. Someone's behavior—the words said or unsaid, the things done or not done—feels wrong to us, and when we feel wronged we feel hurt. We mistakenly connect anger with violence, when *anger is really about being hurt*. When we experience hurt, we often feel angry about it. Let's look at some examples.

- Derek doesn't show up at the mall at the time he and Nick were supposed to meet each other. In fact, he doesn't show up at all! They were planning to hang out for a while and then go to a movie. As Nick waits and waits he feels frustrated, impatient, confused, and eventually hurt. Nick *knows* he had made these plans with Derek! Where is he?! The hurt Nick feels becomes anger toward Derek for failing to honor the commitment they had made.

- Sarah's close friend, Nicole, has said something about her to someone else that has really hurt Sarah's feelings. Her hurt feelings also become angry feelings. She wonders, "How could she have said this?!! I thought we were so close!! I am *so* hurt! I hate her for what she said about me!"

- Reggie gets a test paper back on which he earned a <u>C</u>. His thoughts may go like this: "I thought I had studied really hard, and I was *sure* I was going to get *at least* a <u>B</u> and maybe even an <u>A</u>! What did I get—a lousy <u>C</u>! Why study?! I can't ever get a decent grade in this class!!" Reggie's hurt feelings about his grade quickly become anger at himself, his teacher, the class. . . .

These are just three examples which show how anger and hurt are closely related. When we are hurt—or think we have been hurt—by another, we tend to feel angry.

Think of one experience you have had of feeling angry because someone's words or actions really **hurt** *you. Describe the situation.* _____

_____

_____

_____

_____

_____

Nick, Sarah, Reggie, and you have all felt anger because of how you were hurt. What should you do with these angry feelings? Instead of choosing the old, unhealthy ways of expressing anger, let's look at some alternative ways for dealing with our anger.

TEN PRACTICE SKILLS FOR HEALTHY ANGER EXPRESSION

The practice skills for coping with anger in this chapter are just *some* healthy ways to handle anger. As you read, I invite you to think about how you might be able to apply some of the ideas to specific situations and specific people in your life. All ten practice skills are probably not going to appeal to you, but hopefully, one or more will excite and ignite you on your journey into the land of *Healthy Anger Expression*.

<u>Practice Skill #1</u> **Because you know that anger is often about being hurt or wronged, try to discover *why* you feel hurt.** Ask yourself when you feel angry: "What behavior—words or actions—hurt me?" Sometimes we may be feeling hurt and angry at ourselves for something we did or failed to do. When we have identified the underlying hurt, we can then choose to take some steps toward resolving our angry feelings. We ask: "Who hurt me?" "What, specifically, did he/she do or not do that hurt me?" "What, specifically, did he/she say or not say that hurt me?" "Did I do or say something to hurt myself?"

<u>Practice Skill #2</u> **When you feel anger, your thinking almost always becomes cloudy and unclear, so take some time to cool down and regain clarity of thought.** Anger so often distorts and clouds our thinking. Because our thinking is so unclear when we feel angry, we often say or do things we later regret. When you and I can take some time to cool off—whether it is ten seconds, a couple of minutes or hours, a few days, or longer if need be—we can make a much more conscious and *thought-full* choice about how to express and resolve our anger. By taking this time, we let the impulsive desires to hurt or retaliate or destroy leave us. By taking some time to cool off, the *hurt-full* words and actions that are ready to leap out at someone are less likely to be spoken or acted upon. We are like a coach who calls a time-out when her team is playing poorly. The time-out can help her team regroup and play better. When we take time-out, we regroup and regather ourselves so that we can make a better choice in expressing our anger.

<u>Practice Skill #3</u> **Because anger is energy, seek some physical ways to release this energy.** We just mentioned how our thinking tends to become very unclear when we first feel anger. One way to clear up our thinking is to engage in some physical activity. We want to release our anger energy before it becomes too destructive to ourselves or others. Here's an image to help convey this:

Anger is the air.   The balloon is us.   We strive for healthy ways   Too much air (anger)
                                            to release the air (anger).   and we explode (rage).

You and I can choose from a wide variety of physical activities to help release our anger pressure: walking, running, swimming, basketball, volleyball, football, soccer, dancing, cleaning, shoveling . . . or we may choose to "beat up" our pillow or punch a laundry bag filled with old clothes and sheets. Engaging in some physical activity is a great way to release the anger energy so our balloon doesn't pop.

What physical activities could you engage in to help reduce your anger pressure? _____

_____

_____

_____

_____

_____

Practice Skill #4 Write down your angry thoughts and feelings on paper. Writing is a very powerful tool that will be mentioned in all the chapters to follow. When we write down our angry feelings, we are moving them *out* of us onto the paper. We are defusing the power of our anger and, again, regaining some clarity of thought. When we write, we can be very open and honest about how we feel because no one is going to read it except us. We can choose to rip up and throw away what we wrote after we are done.

Practice Skill #5 Talk to someone who is not the target of your anger and receive some advice and feedback and perspective. Because our thinking is less than clear when we feel angry, we can talk about our situation with another person who has more clarity of thought than we do. This way we are getting someone else's *clear* brain to help our *unclear* brain see things more clearly. We are people who need each other—especially when we are feeling upset!

Practice Skill #6 Talk with your friend, God. Sometimes there might not be anyone available to talk to about our hurt and angry feelings. We do have one Friend, however, who is *always* available to us and who cares very much about how we feel. Our God wants us to choose wisely and well, and sharing our angry feelings with God helps us tap into God's power and wisdom. In fact, we can give God our rawest and wildest anger; we don't have to censor it. God, better than any human being, can receive our temper tantrums and still love us *as we are*. Sometimes when we feel extremely angry, it is almost impossible to pray and communicate with God. In that case we can try to pray when our anger has subsided a bit. We might choose to go for a run or walk and work off some of our anger energy and *then* try to talk with God in prayer. When we turn to God in prayer, we can be completely open and honest with what we say and feel.

Practice Skill #7 Remove yourself from a potentially explosive situation when it is possible and appropriate. When we feel the urge to say hurtful things or when we feel like we might lose control of our anger, it can be very healthy and appropriate to remove ourselves from the situation. This is similar to practice skill #2 in that we are taking some time out, but we are also adding some *physical distance* between ourselves and the person or people we are feeling anger toward. It's very hard to say things we might regret when we have temporarily removed ourselves from the person(s) or situation. We can say, "I'm really feeling angry and I'm afraid I will say some things I'll regret! I'm going for a ten-minute walk in order to cool down. Let's talk about this later." The other person would probably have a lot of respect for us for making such a wise choice, and would much rather have us leave for a little while and cool down rather than listen to our hurtful words. We need to be careful *not* just to walk away without telling why we are leaving. And we need to be sure to come back when we have calmed down a bit to continue working toward resolving the conflict. Leaving the situation temporarily is like a time-out. The "game," the conflict, must be returned to and dealt with.

Name two or three situations of conflict in your life in which it might be wise and healthy to leave for *a while when an argument or disagreement gets heated.* _____

_____

_____

_____

Practice Skill #8 Whenever possible, address the anger—how you have been hurt or wronged or *felt* hurt or wronged—with the person involved. This is one of the harder skills to practice but also one of the most rewarding. Jesus invites us to become reconciled with one another. Reconciliation does not just happen; it takes some effort. Here are a few guidelines to help us become reconciled with people who have hurt us:

1) Practice one or more of the previous seven practice skills so that your anger energy has been reduced and your thinking has become clearer.

2) Spend a few minutes in prayer to ask for God's help in addressing your hurt and angry feelings with the other person(s) involved. God is very eager to help you reconcile.

3) When you talk to the other person

   A) choose to be direct. (In our earlier example, Nick might say, "Hey Derek, have you got a couple minutes?")
   B) choose to be respectful. (We know that we hurt and anger others, so we choose to approach Derek with the same respect we would want others to approach us with when we have hurt them.)
   C) choose to use "I statements" about our feelings. ("*I felt really hurt and angry* when you didn't show up at the mall the other day.")
   D) choose to focus on the other person's behavior rather than personhood. (So Nick doesn't call Derek any names. Instead, he names what Derek did or didn't do that left him feeling hurt or angry. "*When you didn't show up at the mall . . .*" tells Derek about his behavior.)

Pretend you are Erin in the following scenario. Erin is fifteen and has a thirteen-year-old sister, Katie. One evening when Erin returns from basketball practice she finds Katie in her room reading her diary. She is filled with anger toward her younger sister! With what old, unhealthy way(s) might Erin first be tempted to react toward her sister? _____

After she gets her diary back, which of the previous practice skills could help Erin work off some of her initial anger? _____

_____

_____

_____

When Erin finally gets to the point of being able to talk to her sister without screaming at her, how can she be direct, respectful, use "I" statements, and focus on Katie's behavior?

Direct: _____

Respectful: _____

"I" statement: _____

_____

Katie's behavior: _____

_____

When we are angry at another person's behavior, our goal is *not* to talk as calmly as we would when commenting on the weather: "It sure is a nice day." We can have an angry tone to our voice and the person should be able to see and hear that we are feeling angry and hurt. What we want to *avoid* are the old unhealthy ways of expressing anger. We can express our anger and hurt without yelling and screaming. The amazing thing is that when we express our anger more calmly and with more thought behind it, we *communicate* more clearly. Erin, by putting into practice some of the skills for healthy anger expression, will be able to *communicate* more clearly to her sister that it is <u>not</u> okay for her to ever read her diary without her permission!

<u>Practice Skill #9</u> **Show a willingness to admit your fault or part in the conflict.** Usually, though not always, both parties have a part to play in a conflict. Maybe Katie was choosing a poor way to repay Erin for something hurtful Erin had done to her. If this is the case, then Erin definitely needs to hear about how her behavior—whatever it was—hurt Katie and to apologize for it. In the case of our earlier example of Sarah's friend, Nicole, saying something unkind about her, Sarah may have done nothing to "deserve" this. But if Sarah, like most of us, can recall how she has sometimes talked unkindly about others, that may help her to become reconciled with Nicole. Our goal is to work toward reconciliation whenever possible. If someone continues to hurt us with their words or behavior after we have brought this to their attention, we would be wise to step back from the relationship a bit. We do not have to be someone else's "punching bag"—verbal or otherwise—in life.

<u>Practice Skill #10</u> **Show a spirit of forgiveness.** How much easier it is to forgive another person if he or she is truly sorry, than when we get no apology! What a great friend, parent, sibling, teacher, or coach we have if he or she can admit how they have hurt us and apologize to us! We certainly have a

relationship worth hanging on to! Plus, when we forgive others, we can more readily ask others to forgive us when we hurt them.

C H A P T E R   R E C A P

1) Anger is an emotion that most people have some difficulty with. Either we're not very good at expressing our angry feelings or not good at receiving other people's anger.

2) Anger is about hurt. We tend to feel angry when we have been hurt.

3) Ten practice skills (ps) to help us express our anger in healthy and positive ways are:

ps 1   Since anger is about hurt, we try to discover why we feel hurt.
ps 2   Our thinking tends to become unclear when we feel anger, so we take some time-out.
ps 3   Because anger is energy, we seek some physical ways to release it.
ps 4   We can choose to write down our angry thoughts and feelings on paper.
ps 5   We can choose to talk to someone who is not the target of our anger, in order to get some feedback.
ps 6   We can choose to talk with our friend, God.
ps 7   We can choose to remove ourselves from the situation when possible and appropriate.
ps 8   We can choose to address the anger, our hurt, with the other person whenever possible.
ps 9   We can choose to admit our part in the conflict.
ps 10 We can choose to show a spirit of forgiveness.

For Reflection, Journaling, or Discussion

1) Do you agree that most people have a difficult time with anger? _____ Do you think adults need help in expressing their anger in better ways? _____ Explain._____

_____

_____

2) Which of the ten practice skills do you think you will be most likely to try? _____

_____

Which practice skill do you think could help you deal with your anger but would also be hard for you to do? Explain why it would be hard for you. _____

_____

3) What's the hardest or scariest aspect of trying to work out your angry feelings with a person who hurt you?

_____

_____

CHAPTER FOUR

▲ ▽ ▲ ▽ ▲ ▽ ▲ ▽ ▲ ▽ ▲ ▽ ▲ ▽ ▲ ▽ ▲ ▽ ▲ ▽ ▲ ▽ ▲ ▽ ▲

Rage: Sometimes I Just Blow Up!

INTRODUCTION TO RAGE

The dictionary defines rage as "violent anger, violence of feeling." While anger is often about hurt, rage is about violence. We sometimes mistakenly think anger and violence are connected, but the truth is that rage and violence go together. It is really rage and *rage-full* behavior in ourselves and others that frightens and troubles us more than anger does.

Rage is when someone goes out of control. Someone's words and/or actions, whether our own or another's, become violent and destructive. Rage, when it comes on—and it often comes on when we don't expect it—quickly goes out of control.

The anger we feel is like a thunderstorm, whereas our rage can be compared to a tornado. Obviously tornadoes are much more destructive than thunderstorms. Once the harmful energy of rage is released from within us, it is hard to pull it back in, just like a tornado's destructive and violent energy is uncontrollable. Because rage is hard to regain a handle on once it is released, we need to learn to recognize the signs of developing "rage clouds" within us. Meteorologists are trained to recognize the signs that indicate the potential for tornadoes to develop. We can train ourselves to watch for the signs that rage is building within us and take action to defuse our *inner* storms before they become *outer* rage. In the previous chapter we used a balloon to represent us and the air in the

28

balloon to symbolize our anger (see page 23). We want to learn to recognize when rage is growing within us, when we are becoming too filled with anger pressure, so that we can take some steps to decrease our rage before the balloon (us!) pops.

FIVE ESSENTIAL FACTS WE NEED TO KNOW ABOUT RAGE

1) **Rage builds when you don't express your feelings—particularly your feelings of anger, frustration, annoyance, irritation, and the like.** Rage develops when we bottle up our emotions inside us. We can only keep so much frustration and anger inside us before we blow, just like a bottle can only hold so much liquid before it spills out and a balloon can only hold so much air before it pops. When our anger energy is not being released regularly enough (not being expressed), it accumulates and eventually turns into rage. The "age" in "r<u>age</u>" is a good reminder that it is old "stuff" that has built up in us.

2) **Because rage can be such a difficult emotion to recognize before it explodes, you can expect to make progress <u>and</u> experience setbacks as you struggle to express it healthily.** As with all other skills, we do not start out at the mastery level of recognizing and defusing our rage. We need to allow for mistakes, because we *are* going to make them. If rage has been a difficult emotion for you, it will *not* magically become an easy emotion overnight. You will make progress, and you will make mistakes at times. Learning tends to have a "two steps forward, one step backward" rhythm to it. Oftentimes, our one step backward (our failures and mistakes) leads us to making even more progress in handling our rage (the next two steps forward)!

Name any area of your life in which you failed many times before you succeeded. It may be a skill in a particular sport, a school subject, a musical challenge, a hobby. . . . In the space below tell how you experienced the "two steps forward, one step backward" rhythm to learning. _____

_____

_____

_____

3) **When you do have a rage episode, your rage is almost never about the event or person who set you off.** That one extra breath of air (anger, frustration, irritation . . .) into our balloon (us) is the one that releases and unleashes all the old, unexpressed feelings that have built up inside us. There was a whole lot of air (anger, frustrations, irritation . . .) in our balloons before that last event or person who finally was the catalyst to us exploding.

It's often some little thing that leads us to blowing up. When we look back on our rage episode,

29

we are usually dumbfounded (and sometimes a little sheepish) that we got so upset over something so little or so insignificant. I remember one incident when I had a rage attack because I couldn't find my belt. My rage wasn't about my inability to find my belt; I had stored a lot of old frustration and anger that finally reached its breaking point when I couldn't find my belt. If I hadn't had a lot of old stuff in my balloon, my frustrating belt search would not have resulted in rage. I would have just felt frustrated—not rageful.

What are some "little things" you have become extremely upset and angry about in the last year or so?

_____

_____

_____

Do you think you had a lot of stored feelings inside you that might have led to you feeling so upset? Explain.

_____

_____

_____

4) **Anger expression (healthy or unhealthy) and rage attacks seem to be more accepted in our society when they come from males rather than from females.** For some reason, it seems to be more acceptable for men to be angry—and rageful—than it is for women. While there are some differences between the sexes, we have much in common as well. Girls and women are *just as entitled* to their anger and rage as are boys and men. The challenge is the same for both sexes: that of learning how to express our anger and rage in *healthy* ways. So if you are a young woman, please know that feeling angry and rageful is perfectly okay. It is part of being a human being.

5) **Because teens are experiencing so many changes—physical, emotional, intellectual, psychological, and relational—and are having so many different feelings, some of which are quite intense, you can expect to experience rage more often than when you are an adult.** The teens years are filled with changes! The number of feelings you have in one day and the intensity of many of your feelings is, quite naturally, going to lead to some emotional buildup. Plus, many teens are so busy with school and homework and sports and social activities, not to mention how stressed out and physically tired you get—it's no wonder rage can arise from within you! If you find yourself screaming at a family member or feeling very happy one minute and down in the dumps the next minute, you are a perfectly normal teen. If you are feeling ashamed because you really lost your temper with someone, just remember that the

up-and-down nature of your emotions *will* level out. Don't give up on yourself! Keep practicing some of the practice skills in this chapter and the previous one and you <u>will</u> get better at handling your rage.

*Take a moment and write down all the activities you are involved in and the responsibilities you have during the course of a week. (Is it any wonder that you might often feel quite crabby, irritable, and even rageful?!)*_____

_____

_____

_____

_____

_____

SEVEN PRACTICE SKILLS FOR DEALING WITH AND DEFUSING RAGE

<u>Practice Skill #1</u> **Try to determine your level of rage, which will help you decide what self-care actions you need to take.** For instance, if you are at a 9 or 10 on the scale below, you need to get lots of physical activity right away. If you are at a 1 or 2, you are at a very safe level.

RAGE-O-METER

9 or 10 means we are going to have a rage attack very soon. We need to take <u>immediate</u> action. We are like a ticking bomb!

7 or 8 means we are still very high on the scale. We also need to take some action fairly soon to reduce our rage level.

5 or 6 means our rage is at a moderate level. A rage attack can still surprise us at this level. We need to be aware of our rage increasing.

3 or 4 means we are pretty mellow. Rage can still surprise us at this level but it is much less likely than at the higher levels.

1 or 2 means we are very mellow and centered. Rage attacks are very unlikely to occur when we are at this level.

This scale is just an approximate guideline to help us assess our level of rage. We can develop a pretty good sense of where we are on this scale by noticing how easily upset we get, how frustrated and irritable we become, and by paying attention to how violent we may feel (the desire to throw something or hit, for example).

We may also choose to personalize this scale—in other words, to match the different numeric levels with personal behaviors and feelings that give us a clearer indicator of where we're at. For instance, if you are taking things too personally and finding yourself getting easily upset and frustrated, this

31

may mean you are in the 7 to 8 range on the scale. If you find yourself screaming at your little brother or sister, you may be in the 9 to 10 range.

I have learned that I need some quiet time each day to avoid getting overly stressed out, which can set me up for potential rage. You, too, can learn what your signs are of developing rage and what you need to do to take care of yourself.

What are some of the signs and signals that rage may be building in you? _____

_____

_____

<u>Practice Skill #2</u> **If you are very high (9-10) or moderately high (7-8) on the rage-o-meter, you need to seek some physical release right away.**

2a) Again, sports, walking or running, or some other physical activity is a healthy way to decrease our rage levels. It can be especially helpful if you get a good cardiovascular workout. Get those lungs and heart working hard!

2b) You might choose to set up a punching bag to beat on. Because rage is connected to violence (sometimes we feel the urge to break things or slam doors, to scream or yell or use profanity, to hit and to hurt), we release this violence by physically beating on an inanimate object that we can't hurt and that won't hurt us. This does NOT include younger brothers or sisters!!

2c) While beating on your punching bag or pillow, verbalize what needs verbalizing. Words can be very violent and this is the time to get our violent words *out* of us and direct them toward the object we are hitting. We can imagine we are saying them to a real person and it is okay to get real extreme with this. In fact, the more we can get *into* it, the more rage will move *out* of us and we needn't fear going off on someone. It is far better to express our violence—whether it is physical or verbal or both—to a punching bag or pillow than it is to a real person!

<u>Practice Skill #3</u> **Develop an emergency plan with the person or people who have usually received your rage.** Oftentimes it will be one of your parents who can be most helpful. You might sit down with them and tell them you do not want to take your rage out on them any more. Together you might discuss the following:

3a) Gather as much information as possible about your previous episodes with rage. We do this information gathering when our rage level is fairly low and our ability to think clearly is very high. We know we have had rage attacks in the past, and we *will* have them again unless we analyze what triggers our rage and *make a plan* for how we want to try to deal with it. The questions that follow give us some idea of what we should be asking during this information-gathering stage:

"What has triggered my rage attacks in the past?"
"Where has it happened before?"
"What are the situations? the time of day? the day of the week?"
"Who is usually involved?"
"Do I tend to be experiencing more stress and pressure when I have had my rage attacks?"

Where, when, and with whom are you most likely to experience rage? _____

_____

_____

_____

3b) Develop a plan from the information you gathered in 3a. For instance, I know that I am more likely to have a rage attack later in the week because I am more tired. When I feel like a rage attack is about to happen, I tell my wife that my rage level is very high. I also tell her I am going to leave the house for a while—maybe go to the store or go for a walk. When we temporarily remove ourselves from the places we have usually had our rage attacks—and for most teens and adults it is our homes—we are taking a positive step toward handling our rage. If we leave our homes for a little while, we are changing the environment that is contributing to our building rage. If you feel like you are going to scream at your mom or dad, you can choose to go for a walk around the block, where you won't be able to explode at them—because you left them in the house or apartment! If a sibling is getting on your nerves, you can also choose to remove yourself from his or her presence—especially if they keep invading your space. Or if you are experiencing frustration with something you are working on (such as algebra), taking a break can keep you from breaking out into rage. A change of environment changes the stimulus (what is upsetting to us). This allows the upswing emotions (rage) to go down. By leaving for a while, we have moved from a reactive stance (where we react to the things and people around us) to a proactive stance (we choose to *not* let the people and things around us set us off).

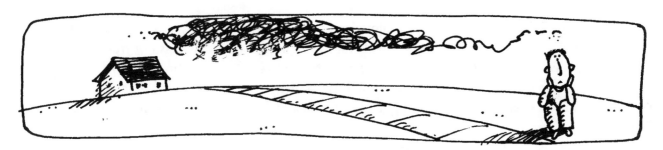

3c) Let the people involved know what your emergency plan is. By letting others know that we need to leave for a while because our rage is building, we are giving them information that things are getting out of hand. We don't just take off without telling why. While we walk around the block and get a breath of fresh air, the people we live with can do their part to de-stress the situation. Maybe a difficult discussion or argument can be continued tomorrow when all the people involved have regained their emotional balance.

<u>Practice Skill #4</u> **Learn to recognize some of the clues and triggers that lead to rage building within and let people know where you are at.** As we have already learned, rage results from <u>old</u> stuff that has built up within us. We *never* express all our emotions, so there will always be a tendency for emotional buildup, rage buildup. Here are some factors that lead to rage buildup in many of us:

- being overextended   • trying to do too much   • no down time or relaxation time
- not enough sleep   • stuffed emotions   • feeling disconnected from others or ourselves
- stress   • too much chaos   • too much noise   • too much activity
- lots of violent or vindictive thoughts   • feeling irritable   • frustration

When we recognize some of these warning signs, we can choose to work toward releasing some of our emotional buildup before it explodes into rage. We can also tell other people what we are feeling so they don't have to guess. Too often, people of all ages expect others to know what is going on inside them when they have never communicated what they are feeling and thinking! It can be very helpful for us and for them to say something like, "I feel really irritable and crabby today!" The chances are the other person(s) will *not* try to irritate us, and we can choose to either get some rest or work through these feelings in some other healthy ways.

<u>Practice Skill #5</u> **To avoid rage explosions, practice anger expression more often.** One of the best things we can do to reduce or avoid rage is to get angry more often! If we express our anger *when* we feel it rather than stuffing it inside, we are less likely to have rage attacks. If we keep stuffing our anger, it <u>will</u> build into rage. When someone hurts you and you feel angry about it, let them know. Move your anger out of you before it becomes rage. (Refer to chapter three for some tips on how to express your anger.)

<u>Practice Skill #6</u> **Seek professional help to assist you in learning the skills to work through your rage and/or to address some deeper problems that may be contributing to your feelings of rage.** Sometimes we carry huge wounds in life that call for professional care. Consistent feelings of rage may be a sign that we need the help of a counselor or pastor. I have sought out professional counseling in my life when I have needed it. I hope you will too. As I experienced healing, I was better able to choose and practice healthier emotional responses.

<u>Practice Skill #7</u> **You need to expect to blow it at times; accept yourself, and treat yourself gently when you fail.** Shame may tell us we are "bad" for having a rage attack. This is <u>not</u> true at all! We are good, yet *imperfect human beings* who are trying the best we can. We wouldn't beat up a tornado victim whose house has been destroyed; nor should we beat up ourselves when we have exploded with rage. Instead, we reassess ourselves in light of the rage attack, make the necessary changes, and try again.

No one handles anger and rage perfectly; neither will you and I. It is very exciting to make some progress, and it is very human to experience some setbacks and failures. We needn't be surprised when we fail. At such times, we really need to be kind to ourselves. We need to forgive ourselves and ask others to forgive us. When we are gentle with ourselves, we can quickly pick up the pieces and try again.

What are some specific ways you can be gentle and kind to yourself after having a rage attack? _____

_____

_____

_____

_____

1) Rage is violent anger, violence of feeling. Just as anger and hurt are connected, rage and violence are connected.

2) Rage can be compared to a tornado, whereas anger is more like a thunderstorm.

3) Our goal with rage is to learn to recognize signs of building rage and take action to defuse it.

4) Five essential facts we need to know about rage are

- Rage builds when you don't express your feelings—particularly feelings of anger, frustration, irritation, and so on. The "age" in "rage" is a reminder that rage is about old stuff that has built up.
- Because rage can be such a difficult emotion to recognize before it explodes, you can expect to make progress and experience setbacks as you struggle to express it in healthy ways.
- When you do have a rage episode, your rage is almost never about the event or person who set you off.
- Anger expression (healthy or unhealthy) and rage attacks are more accepted in our society when they come from males rather than females. It is okay and healthy for girls and women to feel anger and rage. The challenge for both sexes is to express it in constructive ways.
- Because teens are experiencing so many changes—physical, emotional, intellectual, psychological, and relational—and are having so many different feelings, some of which are quite intense, they can expect to experience rage more often than when they become adults.

5) Seven practice skills (ps) for handling and reducing your feelings of rage are:

ps 1   Try to determine your level of rage on the rage-o-meter and take self-care actions.
ps 2   If you are very high or moderately high on the meter, you need to seek physical release.
ps 3   Develop an emergency plan with the person(s) who has usually received your rage.
ps 4   Learn to recognize when your rage levels are rising and let those around you know.
ps 5   To avoid rage explosion, practice anger expression more often.
ps 6   Seek professional help to develop rage-coping skills or to address deeper wounds.
ps 7   Expect to blow it at times; accept yourself, and treat yourself gently when you fail.

For Reflection, Journaling, or Discussion

1) Do you think that analyzing the factors around rage attacks and developing an emergency plan is a realistic and doable goal for most teens and their parents (see ps 3)? Is there a need for such a plan in your family? _____

_____

_____

_____

_____

_____

2) What ideas from this chapter are most helpful to you? _____

_____

_____

_____

_____

_____

3) Does it help to know that many other people—including the author of this book—have had rage attacks too? Why or why not? _____

_____

_____

_____

_____

_____

CHAPTER FIVE

▲ ▽ ▲ ▽ ▲ ▽ ▲ ▽ ▲ ▽ ▲ ▽ ▲ ▽ ▲ ▽ ▲ ▽ ▲ ▽ ▲ ▽ ▲ ▽ ▲ ▽ ▲ ▽ ▲

Through Fear, Into Trust: Why Am I So Afraid?

INTRODUCTION

One of the most uncomfortable and painful feelings we can experience is fear. We tend to resist fear more than most emotions. When we feel fear we often try to get rid of it right away, because it is such an unpleasant feeling. But fear, like most of the emotions, acts as a messenger and is not likely to move on until we listen to its message.

The dictionary defines fear as "a distressing emotion aroused by impending (about to happen) pain, danger, evil, etc., or by the illusion (false impression) of such." Fear has lots of synonyms: abhorrence, anxiety, dread, foreboding, fright, horror, jitters, panic, phobia; we describe someone with fear as scared, nervous, shaky, worried, apprehensive, alarmed, petrified, shook, uneasy, terror-stricken. . . . The fact that fear has more synonyms than most other emotions indicates how troubling this emotion can be. We need many different words to describe the variations of fear we can feel.

Fear, like all emotions, has a range of intensity from very mild to very deep. When we feel fear at its mildest level, we might be slightly worried about something. At its deepest level, we may be in a state of crippling panic or terror. Whether mild or intense, fear is an unpleasant emotion to experience. Obviously, the more fear we feel the greater is our discomfort and pain. The picture of the fear pit at right can help illustrate this point. Our milder fears are closer to the surface of the pit and are easier to face and overcome. Our more intense fears go much deeper, and it takes more courage to face them and more tools to help us regain freedom.

Fortunately there is an antidote to fear: TRUST, which is defined as "belief in and reliance on the strength, ability, and sureness of a person, thing, or God." A few synonyms of trust are certainty, belief, confidence, faith, assurance, and a feeling of security. To trust is to depend on, count on, rely on, and place our faith in ourselves, another person, or God. To trust is to have confidence and hope in the one we are trusting. Usually we are in a state of neither total trust nor total fear. In a previous chapter we learned that feelings are fluid and changing all the time. We roam all over the spectrum from deep trust to deep fear depending on what is happening in our lives and how we are choosing to deal with it.

Briefly describe a time in your life when you felt

deep trust: _____

_____

_____

mild worry: _____

_____

_____

deep fear: _____

_____

_____

WHAT ARE WE AFRAID OF?

As our definition of fear implies, we can be afraid of <u>real</u> dangers (pain and evil, for example) or by the fact that we <u>think</u> we are in danger or will face pain. What we fear may or may not actually happen, but our fears *are* real. Here's an example of how I once suffered fear of physical pain, though sometimes the pain I feared never happened. When I was a boy and went to the doctor for my yearly physicals, I was *always* afraid of the pain of shots. I never knew from year to year whether or not I would get shots. As I waited for the doctor and nurse, my fears of getting a shot spiraled around in my mind and grew larger and larger. Some years I was *very* relieved when I didn't have to get any shots!! Yet because I didn't know whether or not I would get a shot, I still suffered the pain of fear. In this case the shots were illusions, not real, *yet my fears were very real.*

Most of us experience many of the same fears. Almost all of our fears can be placed under one of the following five major categories: fear of change, pain, the future, death, or fear itself.

1) **CHANGE.** We may fear changes in our lives because we are leaving the security and familiarity of the known and exchanging it for the unfamiliar and unknown. Three examples of big changes young teens face are: (Add your own on the line below.)

familiar and known and secure	to	the unfamiliar and unknown
junior high	to	high school
old neighborhood and/or city	to	new neighborhood and/or city
parents together	to	parents separated or divorced
_____	to	_____

Usually the bigger the change in our lives the more intense will be our fears.

2) **PAIN.** We tend to be afraid of things (shots) or people that can hurt us physically, emotionally, or psychologically. We could spend a long time making a list of the pain we fear: fighting (physical or verbal), putdowns, rejection, sickness, parents' divorce or separation, loss of friends, changed relationships, abuse, neglect. . . . Pain hurts, so we fear it.

3) **THE FUTURE.** Most of our fears are about tomorrow(s) rather than yesterday(s). You can't be afraid of yesterday's math test (the past), but you *can* be afraid of your math score, which you haven't received yet (the future). Our minds can run away into countless fears about the future: "What will high school be like?" "Will I make new friends?" What if someone wants to beat me up?" "Will my parents get a divorce?" "Will I get in a terrible accident?" "Will I have a good job?" These are just a few questions many teens ask themselves about the future. The future is unknown, and because it is unknown, we can sometimes feel afraid of it.

What are your biggest fears about the near and/or distant future? _____

_____

_____

4) **DEATH.** Of course, death is the biggest unknown. Most people, even people of faith, have some fear of death. "What if my parents die? How will I make it?" "Will my dying be painful?" "Will there be pain after death?" "Will I be punished?" "Will God reject me?" "What if there is no God? What happens then?"

5) **FEAR.** Because fear can be so painful, we sometimes fear it. For those of us who have suffered anxiety or panic attacks, we are afraid of such future attacks. This heading could really fall under the second common fear we mentioned—pain—but fear *of* fear is a different kind of pain that deserves a special grouping of its own.

THE PURPOSE OF FEAR

Fears are <u>not</u> bad even though they are often unpleasant and painful. Like most unpleasant emotions, fears have information for us, messages for us. The "ear" in "f<u>ear</u>" reminds us to listen. Fears want to be heard and responded to. Angels are God's messengers who seek to protect us and keep us safe. Fears can be our "inner angels" who also want to protect us and help us stay safe. That's why it is so important to listen to these "angels."

Some of Fear's Messages for Us:

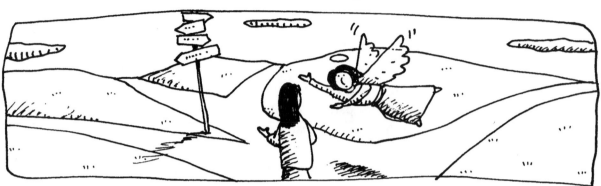

1) **Warning. Go slow, turn around, or stop. You are heading down a potentially dangerous path.** An example might be a relationship that is becoming too serious too fast or one in which there is too much sexual activity. *Add another example:* _____

_____

2) **Be careful. Take care of yourself.** An example might be walking at night. You will want to be sure that drivers can see you and that you are walking with a friend rather than alone. *Add another example:*

_____

_____

3) **You are entering a potentially dangerous situation. Be alert or remove yourself from the situation.** An example might be a party where the parents are not home and there is drinking and/or drug use. *Add another example:* _____

_____

_____

4) **You have done something wrong and are afraid of the consequences.** Your fear angel will visit you with the hopes that you will own up to your mistake and try to correct it whenever possible. An example might be taking something that doesn't belong to you. *Add another example:*

_____

_____

5) **You are experiencing or are going to be experiencing a big change soon.** An example might be you are moving to a new city or state. *Add another example:* _____

_____

_____

6) **You are feeling vulnerable—open to being hurt or rejected—and you need to be protective of yourself.** An example might be you are going to ask a person you have wanted to be friends with if he or she would like to come over sometime, and this person may reject your offer. *Add another example:*

_____

_____

7) **You are taking a risk—the possibility of injury or loss which must be faced in order to achieve a potential gain.** An example might be trying out for a sports team, which you may or may not make. *Add another example:* _____

_____

_____

Our Goals in Dealing with Our Fears

1) **As with any emotion, we don't want fear to run our lives or control us.** Fear that controls us is like a tyrant or dictator. Uncontrolled fear will keep us from taking the risks we need to take in life.

2) **We accept that while we don't want fear to control us, we can't control fear either.** We try to accept fear's visits and consider its messages for us. We let fear come and go like all the other emotions. We try not to fight our feelings of fear, because that only increases their power over us. Fear <u>will</u> come and go regularly throughout our lives.

3) **When unhealthy fear visits us, we give it the boot!** Sometimes our fears are not reasonable, and if left unchallenged will hold us back in some way. We stand up to this fear and challenge it directly.

4) **We try to deal with our fears in one or more of the following five ways:**

Reduce our fears. When we reduce our fears, they are less likely to overpower and overwhelm us.

Manage our fears. When we manage our fears we are in charge of our fears, rather than our fears being in charge of us. To manage our fears means to handle them with skill and authority, the way a baseball manager handles his or her team.

Live with our fears. In many instances we usually live with a combination of fear and trust. For example, our fear of death will always be present in most of us at some level, and so it is a fear we learn to live with. We can improve our ability to live *with* this and other fears.

Face our fears. When we face fear, we can deal with its message. When we run from fear, it gains more power. Our first tendency is often to run from rather than face our fears.

Another image is the storm cloud. Until we face it, it will keep chasing us. Face the fear cloud and the worst that can happen is we get wet as we receive its message. Then we can move on, less fearful.

Grow through our fears. We can ask ourselves: "How have I grown from dealing with my past fears?" "How might I grow from facing this current fear?"

Twenty Practice Skills for Coping with Fear

Practice Skill #1 **We can choose to analyze our thoughts and ask ourselves if our thoughts are rational (reasonable or sensible).** Here's an example of a fifteen-year-old analyzing her thoughts:

Thought: "I'm afraid my parents will die and I'll be all alone."

Feeling: Terror, deep dread, maybe out-of-control fear.

Thought Analysis: "Wait a minute! Are my parents sick? No. Do they look like they are dying? No. Have they told me they are dying? No. So common sense tells me that my parents are not near death. My thoughts are not rational. I will choose to think about something else or do something else."

As a result of this thought analysis and redirection of her attention, her fears reduce dramatically or even completely.

Practice Skill #2 **We can state our reality—what is real—today, right now.** Example: "Today my parents are healthy. I'm healthy. Yes, we will all die someday. I'll deal with it on that day, which is *not* today—HURRAY!"

Practice Skill #3 **Feel the fear and do it anyway.** (There's a book by this title which can be purchased in most bookstores.) Sometimes we have to endure a little discomfort and fear in order to reap the payoff or reward. For example, we may be afraid of going to the dentist, but we choose to endure the temporary discomfort of a dental visit rather than pay a bigger price of walking around with dentures.

Practice Skill #4 **Think of the worst possible thing that could happen in a given situation and then ask if that is very likely to happen.** Example: I have to give a speech in front of a lot of people.

Worst that could happen: My pants will fall down in the middle of my speech. I will lose my place and not be able to find it. Everyone will laugh at me for years. I will never be able to face these people again.

Self-talk: Is that likely to happen? NO.

Practice Skill #5 Proper breathing can reduce our fears in just a couple of minutes. When we inhale our stomach rather than our chest should go out a bit. And when we exhale, our stomach returns to its normal position.

Practice Skill #6 Recite a mantra over and over. A mantra is a word or short phrase (usually eight syllables or less) that is repeated over and over, either mentally or aloud. This can be combined with our breathing. (Remember that your stomach should go out slightly as you inhale and back to its normal position as you exhale.) The words themselves are soothing, as is the repetition. It also provides our minds with a positive focus rather than dwelling upon and increasing our fears. Below are a few examples of mantras that can help us regain inner calm:

<u>Inhale</u> (stomach goes out slightly)   <u>Exhale</u> (stomach returns to normal)

Lord . . . . Jesus
Lord Jesus . . . . calm my fears
God's peace . . . . quiets my fears
The Lord . . . . is my shepherd

Add three more fear-reducing mantras on the lines below:

_____   . . . .   _____

_____   . . . .   _____

_____   . . . .   _____

For mantras to be most effective, they should be practiced regularly so that we can call on them in a time of fear.

Practice Skill #7 Write in a journal or notebook. Writing moves the fear out of our minds and onto the paper, where we can take a better look at it. If we keep it in our minds and continue thinking about it, it spirals around and around and grows deeper and more powerful. The fear becomes trapped in our minds. Writing can help set this emotion free.

Practice Skill #8 Exercise. Maybe we need to stop thinking about our fear so much. We need to make a conscious choice to *stop* thinking about our fear and choose to do something else. Exercise is a healthy way to distract ourselves.

Practice Skill #9 Remind yourself that it is okay to feel afraid and that all people have fears. All healthy people have fears, so the fact that you are afraid at times is a clear indicator of how normal you are. We can say to ourselves: "I'm feeling afraid right now. I don't like this feeling, but I know I am strong enough to feel it. I accept my fear. I know it will move on eventually—especially if I don't cling to it too tightly. I try to hold it with an open hand rather than a clenched fist."

<u>Practice Skill #10</u> **We need to remember that our bigger and deeper fears take a longer time to work through.** For example, a big fear such as the fear of dying may take many years to get a better handle on. It is like being in a long tunnel. Sometimes the tunnel is longer and darker than we would like it to be.

<u>Practice Skill #11</u> **Talking to a trusted person can be very helpful.** This may be a parent, a friend, a teacher, or a pastor or counselor—someone who will show respect for you and your fears. Professionals such as counselors and priests and pastors have special training and a deep understanding of the fears we face in life. They are human beings who also feel fear and have learned some helpful ways of dealing with it.

<u>Practice Skill #12</u> **Dialogue with Jesus back and forth in your journal.** We *do* have the spirit of Jesus within us, so it makes sense that his voice can speak through us. Every time I have written in Jesus' voice I have been helped a lot. Here's a start to a dialogue:

Me: Jesus, I feel so afraid of dying.
Jesus: Do you know why you feel so afraid?
Me: Not exactly. But I think I am afraid you won't accept me.
Jesus: Why do you think that?

<u>Practice Skill #13</u> **Pray any way you can.** Prayer doesn't necessarily take away all our pain, all our fear, but sometimes we feel less alone and regain some inner peace and calm when we give our fears to God. God *will* help us with our fears. God wants us to share our fears so that God can help us.

<u>Practice Skill #14</u> **Read and pray a Psalm from the Bible about trust in God.** For starters you may wish to try Psalms 16, 23, 25, 27, 31, 46. We mentioned earlier that trust is the antidote to fear. These Psalms of trust can help us turn to our God for help when we are afraid. If you are unfamiliar with the Bible, turn to the table of contents in the front of any Bible. The Psalms are located in the Old Testament (sometimes also referred to as the Hebrew Scriptures.) You might want to underline some verses or parts of verses that you find especially comforting and read just those verses over and over slowly—aloud if possible—as you allow God's love to penetrate and break up your fears. Below are some verses from Psalm 16 that I have found comforting and calming when I feel afraid:

verse 5:   *You, Lord, are all I have, and you give me all I need; my future is in your hands.*
verse 8:   *I am always aware of the Lord's presence; he is near and nothing can shake me.*
verse 9:   *I feel completely secure.*
verse 11: *You will show me the path that leads to life.*

Read Psalm 27 and underline the verses or parts of verses that could help calm your fears. On the lines below write the ones you find to be most comforting:

verse _____

verse _____

verse _____

verse _____

verse _____

Practice Skill #15 **Read and pray with some other comforting verses that are found in the Bible.** Did you know the Bible encourages us hundreds of times not to be afraid?! You might want to ask your pastor or priest to help you locate some of these verses. Also, in the back of many Bibles is an index. You might try looking up the words "fear" or "comfort" or "trust" to help locate these healing words. Should you have difficulty finding a particular verse in the Bible, use the table of contents or ask a teacher, parent, or youth director for help. Here are three samples of comforting verses found in God's Word:

Isaiah 43: 1   *Do not be afraid—I will save you. I have called you by name—you are mine.*
Matthew 28:20   *I will be with you always.*
Philippians 4:13 *I can do all things through Christ who strengthens me.*

Some other reassuring verses are found in Appendix 2 on page 90.

Practice Skill #16 **Cling to a Bible verse and let it walk with you and help you throughout the day.** Write it down on a piece of paper. Stick it in your pocket. Read it periodically during the day when you are alone or when no one is looking. As you read it occasionally throughout the day, it will become like healing medicine. Gradually your fears will feel less intense as the verse you chose circulates in your mind and heart.

Practice Skill #17 **Use your imagination and put yourself in a gospel scene or imagine yourself sitting next to Jesus in a peaceful place.** Talk to him. Let him talk to you. Be with him in silence. A possible gospel passage could be the one of Jesus stilling the storm (Mark 4:35–39). Imaginatively place yourself in the boat with Jesus. Tell him your fears and listen for his comforting response. You might combine this with practice skill #12 and have a dialogue with him.

Practice Skill #18 **Write down your fear and place it in a God Box.** A God Box is a symbolic representation for God. It is a way to help us let go of our fear and, with trust, let God hold it. Take a box with a cover, or a can with a lid, and cut a hole in the top big enough to drop a piece of folded paper through. (Coffee cans work great as do some snack food containers that are cylinder shaped.) You might choose to decorate your box or can with pictures—perhaps including a picture of Jesus—so that it no longer looks like a coffee can or snack container. When we write down our fears and drop them into the can or box, we are giving our fears to God.

Practice skill #19 **Have a dialogue with fear. Confront fear directly and ask it what it wants.** If it tries to bully you, stand up to it and tell it that you aren't going to be pushed around. If fear is trying to help you stay safe, thank it for its angelic intervention. (See some of fears messages for us.)

Practice Skill #20 **Try to determine what simple actions you can take to help you with your fears.** You may choose to try one or a combination of the previous nineteen practice skills. Or maybe you will make a list of things you can do about your fears. When we can take some action, regardless how small or simple, we lessen the intensity of our fears.

1) Fear is one of the most painful and powerful emotions we face. The antidote to fear is trust.

2) Most of our fears fall under one of the following five categories: fear of change, pain, the future, death, and fear itself.

3) Fear has many purposes, among which are to warn us to be careful and to be aware of danger.

4) Our goals in dealing with fear are to not let it run our lives; to accept that we can't control fear; to confront unhealthy fear when it tries to hold us back; and to strive to reduce, manage, live with, face, and grow through our fears.

5) Twenty practice skills (ps) for dealing with fear are:

ps 1 Analyze the thoughts that are contributing to your fears to see if they are rational.
ps 2 State your reality—what is real—today, right now.
ps 3 Feel the fear and then do it anyway.
ps 4 Think of the worst possible scenario and then ask yourself if that is very likely to happen.
ps 5 Proper breathing can reduce your fears within minutes.
ps 6 Recite a mantra over and over for a focus place for your mind and a soothing effect.
ps 7 Write down your fears in a journal or notebook. Writing gets our fears out of our minds.
ps 8 Exercise. It is a healthy distraction and a redirection of our energies.
ps 9 Remind yourself that it is okay to feel afraid and that all healthy people have fears.
ps 10 We need to remember that our bigger and deeper fears will take longer to work through.
ps 11 Talking to a trusted person can be very helpful.
ps 12 Dialogue with Jesus back and forth in a journal. His voice is within you.
ps 13 Pray any way you can. Prayer can help us regain inner peace and calm.
ps 14 Read and pray a Psalm from the Bible about trust in God.
ps 15 Read and pray with some other comforting verses that are found in the Bible.
ps 16 Cling to a Bible verse and let it walk with you and help you throughout the day.
ps 17 Use your imagination to place yourself in a gospel scene with Jesus.
ps 18 Write down your fear and place it in a God Box or God Can.
ps 19 Have a dialogue with fear. Confront fear directly and ask it what it wants.
ps 20 Try to determine what simple actions you can take to help you with your fears.

For Reflection, Journaling, or Discussion

1) Look back on your life and identify some fears that you used to have that are no longer fears for you.

_____

_____

_____

_____

2) What are your three biggest fears in life right now? What information from this chapter might help you deal with these fears? _____

_____

_____

_____

_____

_____

3) Interview someone who is at least sixty years old about the fears they have faced in their lives. Did they have some of the same fears at your age that you have? What suggestions did they offer on how to cope with fears? _____

_____

_____

_____

_____

4) Ask your parent(s) what their biggest fears are for and about you? _____

_____

Now write down what your biggest fears are for and about your mom and/or dad. (You may wish to share what you wrote with either your mom or dad.) _____

_____

_____

Do you have some of the same fears for each other? If so, what are they? _____

_____

_____

CHAPTER SIX

▲ ▽ ▲ ▽ ▲ ▽ ▲ ▽ ▲ ▽ ▲ ▽ ▲ ▽ ▲ ▽ ▲ ▽ ▲ ▽ ▲ ▽ ▲ ▽ ▲ ▽ ▲

From Hate to Harmony: How Do I Stop Hating Someone?

INTRODUCTION

Feeling hatred for someone is a guaranteed way to rob us of inner peace. We don't hate a person because we *want* to lose our inner peace and calm; rather it is because we have been harmed—or felt we have been harmed—by this person. Sometimes we spew destructive words upon the person we are hating, which not only hurts them but ourselves as well. Other times we talk about our hate with a friend rather than express it to the person who has harmed us. Still other times, we keep our hate inside us, where it grows like mold in the darkness of our minds.

Whether we express our hate to someone or about someone or keep it in the privacy of our minds, we *pay a price* for hating. If we don't deal with our hate, it ends up consuming us. In this chapter we will attempt to understand hate better—why we hate, its messages for us, and the stages we must pass through on our journey from hate to harmony. We will also identify some practice skills with which we can move out of the "hole of hate" and onto the "hill of harmony," that wonderful place of inner and outer peace.

The dictionary defines hate as "intense dislike of someone or something; hostility; a very strong dislike which is often accompanied by the desire to hurt or harm." Hate is a very powerful and challenging emotion. For Christians, it is an especially troubling emotion, because we are commanded by Jesus to love and forgive one another. Obviously, when we are hating someone, we are not following this command of Jesus. Consequently, we may believe we are "bad" Christians, that we have failed as Christians, and might think that God doesn't love us because our hearts and minds are filled with hate.

The "good news" is our God loves us *unconditionally*. In other words, there are *no* conditions we must meet or live up to in order for God to love us! When we succeed *and* when we fail, we are loved! We are not loved any more when we succeed than when we fail. If anything, it may well be the other way around: our God may love us even more *in the midst of* our failures and broken moments because God doesn't want us to be hurting and unhappy. When you and I are hating someone, we are hurting. Though God loves us just as much when we are hating as when we are loving, we have no sense of God's love. Our feelings of hate tend to overpower and block our ability to enjoy God's love. Obviously, our loving God *wants* us to love because it is a happier and more rewarding way to live. When we are hating, we are unhappy. Mother Teresa has said that we are in this world to love and be loved. It is hard work to love at times; it is not very hard work to hate.

Jesus' teachings to love our enemies, forgive one another, and pray for those who mistreat us *sound* wonderful. Somewhere deep within we know his words are true, yet when we actually try to *live* and *practice* these beautiful teachings, we come face to face with their difficulty. We may even think that what he asks of us is impossible! We may say to ourselves, "Maybe a few really great Christians can love their enemies, but I cannot!"

A wonderful summary of Jesus' teachings are found in the gospel of Matthew, chapters five through seven. This is known as the Sermon on the Mount. Take a few minutes to read these chapters and on the lines below record his teachings that deeply attract you.

_____

_____

_____

_____

It seems like Jesus expects a lot from us! Actually, he is teaching us and offering us *the best way* to be happy in this life. If we want to have the best possible life, it isn't going to happen without a whole lot of effort on our part, just as if we want to be good at a particular sport it will require a great deal of effort and perspiration. You may have had a coach who was very demanding and expected a lot from you. The chances are you also improved a lot under this coach's guidance. So it is with "Coach" Jesus. Jesus is basically saying, "If you want to live a happy and satisfying life, here's what you have to try to do. . . ." Forgiving someone who has hurt us, although very, very tough to do at times, will bring us far more inner peace and happiness than choosing to hang on to our hate and resentment. Forgiving is part of the best possible life!

We can't let go of hate on our own; it tends to cling to us like Super Glue. We *need* Jesus' help and he *needs* our efforts as well. We work *together* as partners—each partner dependent upon the gifts and efforts the other partner brings. If we stay stuck in hate, if we refuse to even *try* to work through our feelings of hate, we become slaves to hate. Hate, rather than our God of love, becomes our master and we become its unhappy prisoner.

EIGHT (ATE) ESSENTIAL FACTS ABOUT HATE

1) Hate, unless dealt with, robs us of our inner peace. This is a great motivator for working toward resolving our feelings of hate. If we want to have inner peace and tranquility, we must *express* and *resolve* our hate. The longer we hate, the longer we go without experiencing that priceless gift of inner peace. The "ate" in "h<u>ate</u>" reminds us how hate will eat away at us, eat away at our peace of mind. The person we are hating lives in our minds and hearts, even though they may not even be thinking of us! The fact that *we* are thinking hateful thoughts about *them*, robs *us* of inner peace! Sometimes we feel unable to stop our hate-filled thoughts, and so hate keeps on feasting upon our insides.

2) When we feel hate toward someone, we cannot instantly stop and rid ourselves of hate. There is a process—a series of steps and stages—we must pass through in order to get out of the hole of hate and onto the hill of harmony. When we decide to walk or run a mile, there are 5,280 feet we must travel *one foot at a time* in order to reach our goal. We know that if we keep walking or running we will eventually arrive at our destination. The same is true when we feel hate. As we keep working and praying our way along the stages we must pass through, we will eventually reach our goal of resolving our hate-filled feelings and regain inner peace. We can't walk or run a mile instantly, nor can we resolve our hate instantly.

3) Hate and inner peace cannot coexist at the same time within us. We have the potential to experience a wide range of emotions. Some emotions can be felt at the same time as other emotions. For instance, we can feel peaceful, thankful, and happy at the same time. Or we can feel angry, hurt, and depressed at the same time. Our feelings don't always come marching along single file like soldiers. Many times, if not most times, they come in twos and threes, with one feeling being more dominant than the others. However, some feelings *cannot* be felt at the same time. We are usually unable to feel trust and terror at the same time. Nor can we feel inner peace and hatred at the same time. We will either feel inner peace or hatred—not both simultaneously.

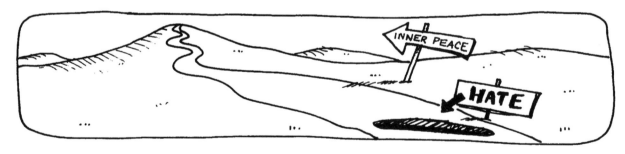

Make a list of emotions that can be felt at the same time. _____

_____

_____

Make a list of emotions that are impossible to feel at the same time. _____

_____

_____

4) The fact that we are able to hate is part of what makes us human. Once more, our unpleasant emotions, while painful and no fun to feel, are part of what makes up our humanity. We can appreciate the feeling of inner peace because we know what it is like to *not* have inner peace. We can value the times we are able to love—including loving our enemies—because we know what is like to hate.

5) Everyone has feelings of hate at some time or another. Some of us struggle with hate more than others. Others of us may struggle with a different emotion, such as fear or anger or loneliness. Most of us have *at least* one unpleasant emotion that is difficult for us, and for some of us it is hate. We needn't feel ashamed when we are feeling hatred. Our challenge, as with all the unpleasant emotions, is to work our way through it.

6) Hate tends to be an intense feeling that sinks deep inside us; thus it has a lot of power and takes more time to heal than many of the other unpleasant emotions. Hate tends to be an emotion we feel very deeply. Because hate is felt deeply, it barges into and wrecks our home of inner peace, which dwells deep inside us. It takes more time to work hate out of our system because it goes deeper than, say, a momentary flash of anger. It is quite literally an uphill climb out of the hole of hate and onto the hill of harmony.

7) While hate comes and goes like all our feelings, we tend to hang on to hate for a long time. Hate would probably move on more quickly if we let it, but we sometimes hold on to it for a variety of reasons that we will explore later in this chapter.

8) Christians are no more immune to feeling hate than people who are not Christians. We Christians are human beings like everyone else and are not exempt from feeling and experiencing any of the unpleasant emotions—including hate. Struggling with guilt because we are Christians who sometimes feel hate is not helpful to our healing. Again, it is a process that takes time and effort and God's presence to help us regain our freedom from the hole of hate.

HATE'S MESSAGES FOR US (WHY WE HATE)

1) Our feelings of hate may tell us that we have been hurt or wronged and that we have some anger to work through. Hate and anger are closely related. The skills we learned for dealing with anger and rage can also help us handle our hate.

2) Hate sometimes tells us that we are afraid of someone or a group of people. Some people hate going to the dentist because they are afraid they will experience pain. Other times we may find it easier and perhaps more acceptable to hate a particular person or a group of people rather than admit we are afraid of them. For example, many people who hate gay people are really afraid of them and/or feel threatened by them. Another example is that we sometimes find it easier to hate people from another country—even though we've never met anyone from there—because of our fears.

Can you name some groups of people whose hate for one other is partly because they are afraid of one other? _____

_____

_____

Have you ever felt hate for a person or a group of people when the deeper emotion has been fear? _____

_____

_____

3) Our feelings of hatred for others is often a sign that we are unhappy with ourselves. We sometimes find it easier to spend our energy hating someone else rather than doing the hard work it takes to make *ourselves* happier. It is very easy to focus on other people and what we may not like in them, when we are really unhappy or dissatisfied with *ourselves.*

4) Hate may tell us that we need to spend some time with God. God is LOVE! God is the healer of all of our wounds and painful emotions. God is a Friend who always accepts us no matter what we are feeling. Sometimes we have some unhealed wounds in our heart that cause us to be unhappy, and when we are unhappy, we are more susceptible to hating others *and* ourselves. God is always one we can turn to in our moments of unhappiness.

5) Hate sometimes tells us that something in someone else—a trait or habit or characteristic—is also in us. Again, it is easier to focus on the *other* person having this behavior or characteristic rather than look at this trait in *ourselves.* For example, I sometimes hate rude people. Part of the reason I hate rude people is because I know that *I can be and have been quite rude at times!* This is a part of myself I really don't like to look at or own, so I find it easier to get upset about other people's rude behavior!

THE SIX STAGES OF HEALING OUR HATRED AND HOW WE CAN PRAY OUR HATE

As was mentioned earlier, the healing of our hate is a process that takes more time than many of our other unpleasant feelings. It may take hours, days, months, years, or even a lifetime to let go of our hate! It depends on the depth of our hate and on our willingness to work and pray our way through it. A formula for healing may go like this:

The Passage of Time + My Efforts + God's Part = Healing

What follows is a rough idea of the six stages we must often pass through on our journey from hate to harmony and healing:

STAGE 1 In this stage intense hatred is our dominant feeling, because the wound we have received is fairly recent. This is the most uncomfortable stage because our feelings of hatred are *so* deep and we may be having violent or vengeful thoughts and fantasies. In this stage hate is eating away at our peace of mind like a lion feasting on a gazelle. Hate is *totally* destroying our inner peace, and we have absolutely <u>no</u> desire to stop hating!

Our prayer in this stage, if we are able to pray, may go like this:

"Lord, I hate James for what he did to me! He is such a jerk! I refuse to stop hating him! I will never forgive him!! . . . "

(This is real prayer, though it may not be how we were taught to pray. It is a good prayer because it is totally honest. It is where we are at—not where we would like to be! God accepts and understands us when we are in this stage! Praying our hate-filled feelings in an open and honest way is part of our healing process.)

And Jesus might say to us in response: *"I understand. I love you right now in the midst of your hate. I'm here to help you when you are ready."*

STAGE 2 The passage of time is absolutely necessary to our healing. In this stage, perhaps a few days or a week or more has passed since we first felt our intense hatred for the person who hurt us. While we still often feel intense hate in this stage—just as deeply and powerfully as in stage 1—we are not thinking about the person *quite* as much. We begin to have a *tiny* desire to let go of our hate because we want to experience inner peace again. We still have very little desire or perhaps no desire to forgive in this stage. We experience an inner tug-of-war: part of us wants to let go of the hate, and the other part of us wants to keep on hating the other person.

If an ice cube represented our hate, in stage 1 we would choose to keep the ice cube in the freezer because we have <u>no</u> desire to let go of the hate in that stage. In stage 2 we would take the ice cube out of the freezer and set it on the counter, but our hate is still hard and has not yet begun to melt.

Our prayer may go like this: *"Lord, I still hate James for what he did to me two weeks ago. I don't want to hate any longer because it robs me of inner peace. But to be honest with you, I still feel a lot of hatred toward him and I really seem unable to stop hating. . . . "*

Jesus might respond with: *"It's okay. It takes time. Even though you don't feel my presence or my peace, I am with you in this hole of hate and I am helping to heal you. Keep on being honest and open with me. Be patient as I am patient. I love you <u>as you are right now</u>."*

53

STAGE 3 More time has passed. We have made more attempts to pray and use some of our other tools for moving hatred and anger out of us. The hate we feel continues to rob us of inner peace from time to time, but we are beginning to have longer stretches when we are neither thinking about nor hating the other person. We want to get out of the hole of hate but recognize we can't do it alone.

Our prayer may go like this: *"Lord, I'm tired of feeling this hate, this resentment, toward James. It's taking its toll on me. I can't stop hating alone. Please help me get beyond this. . . . "*

Jesus might respond: *"I'm here for you. I've been waiting for you to let me help you. This is a big step toward healing that you are taking today by expressing your desire to stop hating. Let me be your strength. . . . "*

STAGE 4 We not only want to stop hating in this stage, but we have some desire to reconcile with the other person. Again it is often an inner tug-of-war: part of us wants to become reconciled with the other person, and part of us wants to keep on holding a grudge. We know that prayer alone will not set us free, especially if it is within our power to reconcile with the other person. (Sometimes we want prayer to save us from doing some of the more challenging things in life, such as making peace with another person. But prayer does not work this way. Prayer is meant to give *us* the strength to *do* the hard things.) We especially need to make some efforts to reconcile if we have a relationship with the other person that we want to preserve. Sometimes we may feel hate toward someone with whom we neither have a significant relationship nor want to have a significant relationship, in which case we are called to make peace with that person in our heart and mind. Our heart, as represented by the ice cube which was taken out of the freezer and placed on the counter in stage two, has begun to soften and melt.

Our prayer may go like this: *"Lord, I am still not totally sincere in my desire to pray for James, but I know that you tell us to pray for our enemies and for those who mistreat us. My heart is really not in it 100 percent, but I still ask that you bless James and help me forgive him. Show me the way to reconciliation."*

Jesus may respond: *"I know it is not easy to let go of hate and reconcile. That's why I am here to help you. You have taken another big step toward healing. I can do so much more for you when you are open as you are now. I am proud of you, and I will continue to show you the way. Trust me."*

STAGE 5 As we become more willing to let go of hate *and* reconcile, we also begin to see *our part* in the conflict or fall-out with the other person, rather than just the *other* person's fault.

We begin to explore our options and choices in dealing directly with the other person when possible. We continue to ask for God's guidance and help.

Our prayer may go like this: *"Lord, I am tired of hate. I've had enough. I've felt it and hung on to it long enough. I think I'm ready for the next step. Please help me. Do you think I should talk to James? . . . "*

Jesus may respond: *"I know that hate has hurt you and robbed you of inner peace. I think since you will be seeing James almost every day at school, it would be a good idea to talk to him. I will help you and be with you. . . . "*

STAGE 6 We make efforts to bring hate to an end, to climb *completely* out of the hole of hate. If we have a relationship with the other person we want to hang on to, we reach out to reconcile. If we don't have a relationship that we want to hold on to, we work toward letting the incident and person go.

Our prayer might be: *"Lord, be with me as I talk to James. Give me the right words, the right tone of voice, and the right timing to say what I need to say. Help me to be truthful and to work toward peace. . . . "*

And Jesus might respond: *"You can count on me to be with you as you approach James. You are so close to healing and I am very happy for you. . . . "*

The stages we just explored are approximations of what we often have to go through to get beyond our hate. It is not an easy process and sometimes there is a repetition of stages. So instead of 1>2>3>4>5>6, it may be 1>2>1>2>3>1>3>4>2>4>5>2>3>4>3>4>5>6. Whatever stage you are in, *know* that our God is with you and is loving you as you are!

THIRTEEN PRACTICE SKILLS TO HELP US GET THROUGH OUR HATE

Practice Skill #1 We need to feel our hatred in all its intensity. Any attempts to shortcut feeling our hate, even though it robs us of inner peace, tends to prolong the process we must go through in order to gain healing. We need to *feel* our hate sooner or later. If we try to stuff it, it will rise again another time.

Practice Skill #2 As with anger, we can choose to pour out our hatred into a letter directed to the person we are hating. We would <u>not</u> mail nor give this letter to the person. Our purpose is to move the hatred out of us a bit, reduce its intensity, so that it has less control of us. We may need to write several such letters over a period of time.

Practice Skill #3 Talking to another person about our hatred can be very helpful. There's something about being heard and understood by another that is *so* helpful to us when we are experiencing unpleasant emotions such as hatred. This third party may be able to give us some helpful advice or feedback.

Practice Skill #4 Analyze the situation and person that is the object of our hate. The use of our minds can be so helpful in regaining control of our emotions. (Remember, we want our minds to lead our emotions and not the other way around.) We try to see what the other person did in behavioral terms—what the person said or did—rather than labeling him or her as a totally bad person. We can ask ourselves:

a) Why do I feel such intense hatred?
b) How was I hurt? What behaviors upset me?
c) Am I blowing this incident up to be bigger than it really is?
d) Am I unhappy or frustrated in my life right now, which might be causing me to be overly sensitive to hurts?
e) What is this hate trying to tell me?
f) What are my choices? How can I choose wisely?
g) Of the six stages of healing, which stage am I in now? How can I take care of myself?

<u>Practice Skill #5</u> **Involve God in your struggle with hate.** We may choose to pray or ask God to sit with us in our hole of hate. God will help us to the extent we provide an opening for God.

<u>Practice Skill #6</u> **Identify and make a plan of some *specific* actions you can take <u>this day</u> regardless of what stage of hate you find yourself in.** When we make a plan of action, we can regain some control of hate. Even if we are in stage 1 and are feeling very intense hatred, we can make some plans so that hate doesn't eat at us *all* day. We can get involved with some other activities to distract ourselves a bit and to have somewhat of a positive day.

<u>Practice Skill #7</u> **Strive for self-acceptance.** Sometimes when we feel hate, especially if we are in stage 1, it is very hard to accept ourselves, because our hate is so intense and we are probably having vengeful and violent thoughts. We can ask ourselves, "Since God loves me even when I am consumed by hate, how can I be loving and gentle with myself this day?" We might choose to do three very kind actions for ourselves: maybe buy ourselves a small gift, just as we would for someone in the hospital; or curl up on the couch and watch a favorite movie; or write a very nice and encouraging letter to ourselves. . . .

<u>Practice Skill #8</u> **Develop a symbolic gesture, ritual, or ceremony to help you let go of hate.** Oftentimes with our most powerful emotions, we need to engage in some type of physical ceremony to help set us free. We might feel a little awkward or silly doing these ceremonies, but no one has to see us perform them. When I use a ritual or ceremony, I do it in such a way that no one sees me. I have always been struck by how much better I feel later in the day after participating in a physical ceremony of some type. Here are three examples of rituals or ceremonies that might help you let go of hate:

a) Write down your hate and express your desire to let it go on a small piece of paper. You might fold the paper or rip it up and bury it in a garden or in a compost pile or under some leaves or even under some snow. The paper itself will decompose and our hate will also begin to break up.
b) Write down the hate you feel toward the other person on a piece of paper. Get all of the hate out onto this paper. Do not censor what you write. Then tear up the paper into tiny pieces and stomp it into the waste basket as a way of *physically* moving the hate out of you.
c) Do a cleansing ceremony. Our hate poisons us and robs us of inner peace, so we might choose to take a small bowl of water, dip our finger in it and trace a sign of the cross on our temple as a symbolic gesture of freeing our mind from hate's grip. We might make the sign of the cross on our tongue and

lips to cleanse ourselves from hurtful words we might want to say. And we can make a sign of the cross on our hearts as a way of healing the hate that has robbed us of inner peace. . . .

Practice Skill #9 **Write down your hate and your desire to be freed from hate on a piece of paper and place it in your Bible next to a scripture passage that is meaningful for you.** This symbolically places it in God's hands. Maybe you could copy down a couple of Bible verses on another piece of paper and exchange the hate you have written down for the healing verses from the Bible. We make a trade with God; we give God our hate and God gives us healing words.

Practice Skill #10 **Enter a scripture story and change and adapt the story to fit the hate you are feeling.** We personalize the scripture passage so that God's Word can heal us. For example, in Mark 3:1–6, Jesus heals a man with a withered and paralyzed hand. In verse five he says, "Stretch out your hand." The man stretches out his hand and it becomes well again. We can imagine ourselves in this story as the person who is paralyzed by *hate*. We can reread this story with ourselves as the person in need of healing. We can imagine Jesus saying to us, "Stretch out your *hate*." As we give our hate to him, we can begin to allow God to transform our hate and decrease its paralyzing and poisoning effect on us.

Practice Skill #11 **Pray for a willingness to let go of hate.** Sometimes we have *no* desire to let go of hate, so we need to pray for a *willingness to let go.* Maybe after many prayers for such a willingness, we might begin to have a *little* desire to let go of the hate we have been clinging to and that has been clinging to us.

Practice Skill #12 **Focus on behavior.** When we focus on behavior, we can see that it was someone's *poor behavior* that is upsetting to us. We also remember how we have behaved poorly at times, which has led other people to feel upset with us. We also look for *our* part in the conflict. Maybe we never told the other person how his or her teasing affected us. Maybe we never let them know that their words and/or actions bothered us. Focusing on behavior helps us to see the other person as simply a person like us rather than as some sort of monster.

Practice Skill #13 **We pray for our "enemy," for the person we are hating.** How do we do this? First of all, to pray for our enemy does <u>not</u> mean we will ever have loving feelings for him or her. Our prayer is not meant to produce loving and warm feelings but rather to help us choose loving and nondestructive actions. We might not feel any love in our heart for the other person, but perhaps we can pray for:

    a) the *strength* to not retaliate.
    b) the *vision* to see that this person is not *all* bad.
    c) the *wisdom* to let go of the person and the incident into God's care.
    d) the *willingness* to let go of hate.
    e) the *humility and courage* to take the first steps to reconcile when possible.
    f) the *desire* to have God love and bless this person in a special way.
    g) the *heart* to forgive.
    h) the *maturity* to take the higher and more difficult path.

CONCLUDING REMARKS

Our greatest motivation for working through our feelings of hatred is to regain the beautiful gift of inner peace. We cannot have **inner peace** until we have **outer peace**.

"So if you are about to offer your gift to God at the altar and there you remember that your brother or sister has something against you, leave your gift there in front of the altar, go at once and make peace with your brother or sister, and then come back and offer your gift to God."

Mt 5:23–24

It is no easy thing to work through hatred! It takes time and effort and God's healing touch. Hopefully, with practice, you and I can let go of our hate a little sooner, save some friendships in the process, and regain the "peace of God which surpasses all human understanding."

CHAPTER RECAP

1) Hate is a difficult emotion, especially for Christians, because we are commanded to love.

2) Eight (ate) essential facts about hate are:

- Hate, unless dealt with, robs us of inner peace.
- When we feel hate toward someone, we cannot *instantly* stop and rid ourselves of our hate.
- Hate and inner peace cannot coexist at the same time within us.
- The fact that we can hate is part of what makes us human.
- Everyone has feelings of hate at some time or another.
- Hate tends to be intense and strong and sink deep inside us. It has more power and takes more time to heal than many other unpleasant emotions.
- While hate comes and goes like all our feelings, we tend to hang on to hate for a long time.
- Christians are no more immune to feeling hate than people who are not Christians.

3) Hate's messages for us and why we hate:

- Hate may tell us that we have been hurt and wronged and we have anger to work through.
- Hate sometimes tells us that we are afraid of someone or a group of people.
- Hate is sometimes a sign that we are unhappy with ourselves.
- Hate may tell us that we need to spend some time with God.
- Hate may tell us that something in someone else—a trait, habit, or characteristic—is also in us, and we prefer to focus on the other person rather than see this in ourselves.

4) There are six stages we often must pass through on our journey from the hole of hate onto the hill of harmony.

5) These six stages do not always go in order; we may need to revisit some of these stages several times.

6) An equation for healing: **The Passage of Time + My Efforts + God's Part = Healing**

7) Thirteen practice skills (ps) to help us get through our hate are:

ps 1 We need to first feel our hatred with all its intensity.

ps 2 As with anger, we can pour our hatred out into a letter directed to the person we hate.

ps 3 Talking to another person who is not the object of our hatred can be very helpful.

ps 4 Analyze the situation and person that are the objects of our hate.

ps 5 Involve God in your struggle with feeling hate.

ps 6 Identify and make a plan of some specific actions you can take this day, so your day isn't totally ruined by hate.

ps 7 Strive for self-acceptance. Try to do some kind actions for yourself.

ps 8 Develop a symbolic gesture, ritual, or ceremony to help you let go of hate.

ps 9 Write down your hate and place the paper in your Bible next to a passage you like.

ps 10 Enter a scripture story and change and adapt the story to fit the hate you are feeling.

ps 11 Pray for a willingness to let go of hate.

ps 12 Focus on behavior. This helps us see the other person as a *person* and not as a monster.

ps 13 We pray for our "enemy," for the person we are hating.

For Reflection, Journaling, or Discussion

1) Of the eight (ate) essential facts about hate in this chapter, which one(s) do you relate with the most? Why? _____

_____

_____

_____

2) How have you worked through your feelings of hate in the past? _____

_____

_____

_____

3) Does it help knowing that there are six stages many of us must go through when we are feeling hate toward someone? Why or why not? If you are feeling hate toward someone right now, what stage are you in? What can you do to begin working your way out of hate? _____

_____

_____

_____

4) Do you think there are some people, such as a family member or a close friend, we should never *feel hate toward? Why or why not?* _____

_____

_____

_____

CHAPTER SEVEN

▲ ▽ ▲ ▽ ▲ ▽ ▲ ▽ ▲ ▽ ▲ ▽ ▲ ▽ ▲ ▽ ▲ ▽ ▲ ▽ ▲ ▽ ▲

Self-Esteem: Where Did It Go? How Can It Grow?

INTRODUCTION

"I hate myself!" "I am *so* ugly and fat!" "I can't do *anything* right!" "I am *so* dumb!" "I wish I was more like _____ . She is *so* smart and pretty!" "I *hate* my body!" "I wish I had *never* been born!"

Does any of this sound familiar? My hunch is that most teens have said very hurtful statements, like the ones above, to and about themselves. For some young people, these critical messages to themselves dominate their waking hours and cause them much inner pain.

When you were a small child, you proudly proclaimed all you *could* do. You may have excitedly announced accomplishments such as the following: "Look at my picture, Mom. Isn't it pretty?" "Watch me ride my bike." "Do you want to see me write my name?" "I can do a cartwheel. Want to see?" "I know how to read." Many of your newfound discoveries and abilities were frequently praised by parents and other adults.

Just a few short years later, however, a young teen's attitude has often changed from "Look at me and all I can do!" to "Don't look at me because I can't do anything!". The young child usually feels special about who he or she is. The young teen often feels special only in how <u>un</u>special and <u>un</u>talented he or she is. The praise so frequently received at a younger age seems to come more infrequently. And when people do praise you now, it is harder to actually *hear and believe* their compliments. It's almost as if teens have an inner shield that bats away and rejects all praise. If, however, someone were to criticize you—whether it be a teacher or parent or peer—you take it deeply into your heart and mind as if it were a great treasure and believe it with all your heart, mind, and soul! Of course the person who talks to *you* the most is *yourself*. If your self-talk is negative and critical, your self-esteem is bound to sink lower and lower.

What are some critical messages you give yourself? What self-putdowns do you say to yourself, either aloud or in the silence of your mind? _____

_____

_____

_____

It's a sad fact of life that human beings of all ages are often heartlessly critical of one another. Even very small children quickly learn this when they venture off to school. Many students, from first graders through seniors in high school, have been criticized and rejected by their peers for a variety of reasons. Perhaps *you* have been rejected by your peers for things about yourself that are beyond your control. Some students have been and continue to be rejected and ridiculed for being too short, too tall, too heavy, or too skinny. Others have been excluded or put down for having different hair or skin color. Some get left out for being too smart, not smart enough, too attractive, not attractive enough, or for failing to be athletic. Still others are tormented for being different in ways that are unacceptable to the majority of kids.

What are some other reasons young people your age seem to get rejected or picked on? _____

_____

_____

_____

I remember when I was in eighth grade and my sister, who was a senior in high school, was named homecoming queen. One of my classmates came up to me and said, "Your sister is so beautiful! What happened to *you*?!" You can imagine how I felt! For much of my life—even well into adulthood—I thought I was ugly! Perhaps if I had had a stronger sense of self-esteem, comments such as the one I received would not have hurt me as much as they did.

But no matter how many unkind things *others* may have said about me, *I* quickly learned and mastered the art of putting *myself* down. Perhaps you, too, are becoming quite skilled at putting yourself down.

Let's conduct a little experiment. You will need a watch or a clock with a second hand or a timer. In one minute write down all the things that are good about you and that you like about yourself. Then take another minute and write down all the things that are "bad" about you and that you don't like about yourself.

What I find good about me and like about myself _____

_____

_____

_____

What I find "bad" about me and don't like about myself: _____

_____

_____

_____

Which list was longer? Which list was easier to make? Did you have to think harder to name your good qualities? Or did your good qualities come quickly to mind? I would be willing to bet that it was far easier to rattle off your supposed "bad" qualities and the things you don't like about yourself than it was to name your good qualities. If you are experiencing a difficult time in your life, it was probably real easy to list your faults and weaknesses. If things are going pretty well for you, perhaps you found it easier to list your good points and strengths.

The information in this chapter is meant to help you improve how *you* feel about *you*. If you are already feeling good about yourself, perhaps something in this chapter will further strengthen your sense of goodness. Before identifying some practice skills with which you can raise your self-esteem or keep it high, let's learn some self-esteem essentials.

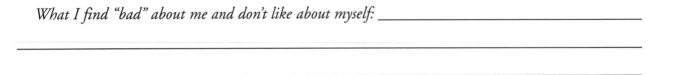

SEVEN BASIC FACTS ABOUT SELF-ESTEEM

1) **Self-esteem is defined as "respect for or a favorable impression of oneself."** Obviously if we have high self-esteem, we have a lot of respect for and a very favorable impression of ourselves. If we have low self-esteem, we don't have much self-respect or a very favorable impression of ourselves.

2) **Teens who have very low self-esteem can gradually improve how they feel about themselves and one day have very high self-esteem.** I had very low self-esteem for much of my life. As an adult, I worked on my self-esteem and now it is pretty strong. Since you are a teen, if you start working on improving your self-esteem <u>now</u>, you can feel better about yourself in the near future and carry this favorable impression of yourself into the exciting years ahead of you!

3) **Low self-esteem takes more work and a longer period of time to heal than almost any other emotion.** We might as well learn this from the start. We have been given by others <u>and</u> have given ourselves a lot of negative messages that have made their home deep within. Like the feeling of hate, which we explored in the last chapter, low self-esteem sinks deep inside us. It takes time to heal the inner damage, <u>and</u> it takes a lot of effort on our part. Time will march on as it always does. The effort will have to come from *you* as you try some of the practice skills in this chapter. The equation we learned for getting through and beyond our hate is the same for raising our self-esteem:

Time + My Efforts + God's Part = Healing (Higher Self-Esteem)

4) **Five major factors that positively and/or negatively impact your self-esteem are parents, peers, your successes and failures, your self-talk, and the media.** We are all imperfect people. Your **parents** are

imperfect and so are you. Sometimes parents wound their children in their imperfect attempts to love them. Perhaps instead of complimenting you, your mom or dad criticizes you. If you have been criticized more than complimented, the chances are your self-esteem is going to be lower than a person who is frequently praised at home. It's important to remember that your parents are *not* trying to ruin your self-esteem. Lots of factors, which are beyond the scope of this book, influence how a parent parents.

A young person's **peers** greatly affect his or her self-esteem. As a teen, your peers begin to have more influence—positive or negative—on you than your parents do. If you hang around negative and critical people, this negativity and criticism will rub off and into you. If your friends have a bad attitude about themselves and life, this attitude will weaken *your* self-esteem. If your peers constantly put you down, you will learn to put yourself down.

If we have had many **failures** in life, there's a good chance that our self-esteem is lower than someone who has had mostly successes in life. Sometimes a young person becomes so convinced that he or she is a failure that they *look* for opportunities to fail, and thus reinforce this sense of being a failure. Failing becomes easy and natural, while success seems to be beyond their capabilities.

We **talk to ourselves** all the time. How many names have we called ourselves? How self-critical are we? Our self-talk is a *huge* factor in how much respect we have for ourselves.

The **media** is one force that has a subtle but powerful effect upon how we feel about ourselves. We are bombarded with "perfect" bodies and faces in commercials, television shows, and magazines. We compare ourselves to these "beautiful" people and often fail to see our *own* beauty. When we fail to see our own inner and outer beauty, our self-esteem plunges.

5) Self-esteem is especially fragile during the teen years because of the enormous changes young people are going through. Just the physical changes alone in young people's bodies can cause self-esteem to be fragile, not to mention all the other emotional, psychological, and relational changes that are taking place! You are at that awkward, in-between stage of life called adolescence: you are no longer a child but not yet an adult. You are a *teen* who is *in-between* childhood and adulthood! This time of your life is full of almost constant changes. And any time there are big changes going on, self-esteem is more vulnerable (capable of being wounded or hurt) and fragile. Lots of coping skills are needed to help you through this exciting yet challenging time of life.

Name all the ways you have changed in the last couple years. You might want to include physical changes, interests, opinions you now have, how you think about yourself, how you view the world, how your relationship with your parent(s) has changed, etc. _____

_____

_____

_____

6) Self-esteem is more vulnerable and fragile during the teen years because tremendous importance is placed on what a teen's peers think of him or her. Because this is a time of such huge changes, teens seek outside approval from others, from their peers. Basically a young person wants to know, "Am I okay? Do you accept me and approve of me?" Teens don't want this acceptance and approval from their parents as much as they do from their peers. Mom or Dad's opinion, while still valued, becomes less and less important in comparison to what a young person's peers think. When you are rejected or excluded or not approved of by your peers, your self-esteem can crumble. When you are accepted, included, and approved of, your self-esteem can soar. Adults, too, want and need approval and acceptance from others, but *not* to the degree that teens do. For teens, this acceptance and approval is of paramount importance.

7) **You have been created in the image of God. You have been created good.** No matter how bad you may feel about yourself, *you are good and valuable in God's eyes and God wants you to be able to see and celebrate your own goodness!*

   "God created human beings, making them to be like himself. (God is good! So are you!) *God created them male and female, blessed them . . . and he was pleased."* (Gn 1:27, 31)

TEN PRACTICE SKILLS FOR RAISING AND STRENGTHENING YOUR SELF-ESTEEM

As mentioned previously, it <u>does</u> take a lot of effort on your part to improve your self-esteem. I had to work very hard to raise my self-esteem. I encourage you to pick two or three or more of the following practice skills and make these activities part of your life. Just as regular practice is needed if you want to improve in a sport or in playing a musical instrument, practice is also necessary in order to improve your self-esteem.

<u>Practice Skill #1</u> **Keep a record of the things you do well each day in a notebook.** When we have poor self-esteem, we often believe we don't do *anything* well. We need to *train ourselves to see* what we do well each day. These can be, and usually are, very "small" things. Small things add up. Here are some examples: *I cleaned my room, I made my bed, I got some exercise, I studied for a test, I called a friend, I helped a friend with a science problem. . . .*

   We start off each phrase with "I" followed by some action. What we are trying to do is get in the habit of seeing the positive and good things we do each day. When we write these actions in a notebook or journal, we are keeping a record of the good we do, compiling evidence, so that when negativity wants to sink our self-esteem, our record of accomplishments can help save our self-esteem ship. On a really low day, we might choose to reread some of our entries in order to see that we have had better days. We might want to start off by writing three positive accomplishments from each day and work our way up to five and then ten. At first it may take you a little while to think of some positive actions you have taken, but with practice, you will train yourself to quickly notice and record the good you do each day.

   *Take a minute and try writing some accomplishments from today or the past couple of days. Remember, they can be little things.*_____

_____

Practice Skill #2 **Write, read, and recite daily affirmations.** An affirmation is a positive statement about ourselves. We use the present tense (I <u>am</u> a good person) when we affirm ourselves, not the past tense (I <u>used to be</u> a good person) nor the future tense (Someday I <u>will be</u> a good person). Here are some examples:

I am beginning to feel better about myself.
I am a good person.
I am loved and lovable.
I am improving in . . .
I am discovering my own good qualities.
I am proud of my ability to . . .

Writing and reciting affirmations is like taking a daily vitamin that helps us heal from all the negative messages we have received from others and ourselves. This is an activity that will only take one or two minutes each day. We might want to choose two or three affirmations and slowly recite each one aloud five times to ourselves. We may choose to look in the mirror as we say these healing messages to ourselves. Below are some phrases with which to begin your affirmations:

I am . . . I am a . . . I am beginning to . . . I am improving in . . . I am making progress at . . . I am developing . . . I am proud of . . . I am beginning to see my . . . I like . . . about myself. God is proud of . . . in me.

When we first try to affirm an area of weakness or something we don't like about ourselves, we might find ourselves not believing the affirmation. That's okay. If we have called ourselves "stupid" for a long time, we are not going to believe right away an affirmation that affirms our intelligence. The "I am stupid" statement has made its home within us and will not be eager to leave. The more regularly we affirm "I am smart" over a period of time, the more we weaken the old, negative message and strengthen the new, positive message.

Write three affirmations in the space below. Say each one to yourself five times.

1) _____

2) _____

3) _____

Practice Skill #3 **Hang out with positive people who respect you and treat you well.** When we are around positive, respectful, and healthy people, it rubs off on us. Some teens (and adults) can only feel better about themselves by putting others down. This doesn't mean we avoid everyone who hurts us, but we want to remove ourselves from chronically negative people and people who may enjoy putting us or others down. Playful teasing comments are one thing; consistent hurtful putdowns are quite another. You need to remove yourself from the latter.

<u>Practice Skill #4</u> **Avoid comparing yourself with others as much as possible.**   It is very human to compare ourselves to others. When our self-esteem is fragile, however, we need to be careful about comparing ourselves to others, because *everyone* seems like a better and/or more gifted person than we are. When we compare ourselves to another person, we are setting ourselves up for low self-esteem. Even if we compare ourselves to another person and decide we are *better* than him or her, this feeling of superiority is <u>not</u> a sign of healthy self-esteem. Our challenge is to see *both* our own positive points *and* the good qualities of others as well.

When you recognize that you are comparing yourself to others and feeling bad about yourself, you can stop and ask, "What are *my* good points? What are *my* strengths? How am *I* improving?" The key is to make a decision to <u>stop</u> comparing yourself to others! Once you have stopped comparing, then you must look for, name, and claim your own good qualities.

<u>Practice Skill #5</u> **Ask others to help you see your good qualities.** It's amazing how blind we often become to our own goodness! We can ask friends, parent(s), or teachers whom we trust for some feedback about ourselves. We might say, "I'm really not feeling so good about myself these days. What do you see that is good in me? What do you think are my strengths and good qualities?" Then our challenge is to listen to them—NOT argue! We might not believe what they are saying about us, and that's okay. We asked for some feedback and these people, who may see us more clearly than we see ourselves, are telling us what *they* see. It would be wise to write what they say about us. Sometimes they point out a good quality of ours in an area we think we are weakest. I once had a friend tell me I was the most forgiving person she had met. I, on the other hand, had always seen myself as a person who doesn't forgive very well or very easily. I was really shocked and blessed by what she said. The chances are that you too will be very pleasantly surprised—maybe even shocked—and blessed by the good others see in you!

Ask three people to tell you the good they see in you—your strengths, skills, and good qualities.

Person's name: _____   *The good he/she sees in me:* _____

_____

Person's name: _____   *The good he/she sees in me:* _____

_____

Person's name: _____   *The good he/she sees in me:* _____

_____

<u>Practice Skill #6</u> **Pick one area for self-improvement and develop a plan for how you can strengthen that part of your life.** You want to pick something that would be a reasonable challenge for you—neither too simple (tie your shoes) nor too hard (learn Chinese in one week). When you identify an area for self-improvement, you want it to be something *you* really want to work at and not something a par-

ent or teacher or someone else wants for you. If *you* want it, you will work harder than if it is something *someone else* wants for you. Some possible examples might include improving in a particular class at school, reaching out to people more or going to more social events, improving in a sport, reading one book a month, or doing some volunteer work. . . . When we stretch ourselves a bit and make a plan for self-improvement, <u>we gain a sense of personal power</u> that positively impacts our self-esteem. We then believe that we can make improvements and positive changes in other areas of our lives!

An area I want to improve in is _____. *Here's how I will go about making improvement:*

_____

_____

<u>Practice Skill #7</u> **Practice "I choose" statements.** When we use the word "choose," we have a sense of power and choice. So often when we have low self-esteem, we say "I can't." Yes, there are many things we can't do—fly a plane, command a submarine, play quarterback in the NFL—but there are many things we *can* do if we so choose. "I <u>choose</u> to practice my affirmations." "I <u>choose</u> to do my homework." "I <u>choose</u> to . . . "

I CHOOSE = PERSONAL POWER   I CAN'T = POWERLESSNESS

People with high self-esteem have a sense of personal power in their lives. Using "choose" helps us develop this personal power!

Make a list of five "I choose" statements that are within your power:

I choose to study tonight. I choose to _____

_____

<u>Practice Skill #8</u> **Develop a plan for the day.** If you want to go to a movie with some friends, you make arrangements. You don't just happen to run into your closest friends by coincidence at the movies at seven o'clock on Friday night! So it is with our daily lives. If we make plans, we have a better chance of having a productive and positive day, which leads to stronger and healthier self-esteem. We can make a daily agenda and try to include some time for the hard stuff we don't like to do (homework, chores, etc.) and some time for things we enjoy doing (watching a favorite television show or talking on the phone, for example). We again develop our sense of personal power and choice when we *plan* our days. As we have productive and positive days, we tend to feel better about ourselves.

<u>Practice Skill #9</u> **Set some short-term and long-term goals.** Imagine a football game with *no* yard markers or end zones! In what direction would the offensive team go? Where would the defensive team try to keep the offensive team from going? How could a team score? This is obviously an extreme example of how having goals are important, not only in the games we play but in all aspects of life.

More than likely you don't know what career you want to have when you are an adult, but you can set other more immediate goals in your life. Your goals may be personal, academic, social, spiritual, physical. . . . You might set a goal of working out four days a week or reading one hour a week or praying three times a week or. . . . <u>Goals give us direction</u>, which we human beings *really* need. We need a direction to head in and a reason for pursuing that course of action. Without goals, we are like a rudderless raft out at sea, unable to choose our direction in life. We just drift wherever the winds and waves blow us. When we work toward our goals, we tend to feel better about ourselves because we have more control of our destiny. When we set goals, we must also make a plan for *how* we will reach them and for *when* and *how* we will evaluate them.

GOALS >> PLANS FOR REACHING GOAL>> EVALUATE>> CELEBRATE>> HIGHER SELF-ESTEEM

Below is an example of a goal that Kara, a ninth grader, set for herself:

Goal: *Be able to run a mile in eight minutes or less, six weeks from today*

Plans for reaching my goal: *Run and walk a mile five days a week for four weeks. Try to run more each week and walk less. The last two weeks I will run only.*

When and how I will evaluate my progress: *I will evaluate my progress by timing myself each day and see how I have improved at the end of every week.*

How I will celebrate if I reach my goal: *Buy myself a CD with my babysitting money.*

Kara may or may not reach her goal, but at least she has <u>set</u> a goal and is willing to <u>work</u> toward achieving it. If she doesn't reach her goal, she can reevaluate the factors that prevented her from making her goal (maybe she suffered from a bad cold for two weeks, which set her back) and try again. There is a very strong chance that she *will* feel better about herself because she has set a goal and is working toward achieving it.

<u>Practice Skill #10</u> **Talk to God in prayer about your wounded self-esteem and pray for healing.** God is the one who created you good and cares very much when you have lost sight of your own personal goodness. When we feel lousy about ourselves, we can bring this to God. We can ask God to show us our good qualities just as we asked other people in practice skill #5. Our time in prayer will help heal our low self-esteem. God has the power and desire to heal us in our most wounded places. God may heal us through other people such as counselors or through affirmations or through a special friend in our lives. . . .

CHAPTER RECAP

1) Some teens are often very critical of themselves. They are masters of pointing out their weaknesses—real or imagined—and not very good at naming their strengths and good qualities.

2) Young people who consistently experience rejection from their peers often suffer from low self-esteem.

3) Seven basic facts about self-esteem are:

- Self-esteem is defined as "respect for or a favorable impression of oneself."
- Teens who have very low self-esteem can gradually improve how they feel about themselves and one day have very high self-esteem.
- Low self-esteem takes more work and a longer period of time to heal than most emotions.
- Five major factors that positively and/or negatively impact a young person's self-esteem are parents, peers, successes and failures, self-talk, and the media.
- Self-esteem is especially fragile during the teen years because of the enormous changes young people are going through.
- Self-esteem is more vulnerable and fragile during the teen years because tremendous importance is placed on how teens relate to and accept one another.
- We have all been created in the image of God. We have been created good.

4) Ten practice skills (ps) for raising and strengthening your self-esteem are:

ps 1   Keep a record of the things you do well each day in a notebook.

ps 2   Write down, read, and recite daily affirmations.

ps 3   Hang out with people who respect you and treat you well.

ps 4   Avoid comparing yourself with others as much as possible.

ps 5   Ask others to help you see your good qualities.

ps 6   Pick one area for self-improvement and develop a plan for strengthening this area.

ps 7   Practice "I choose" statements that give you a sense of power and choice.

ps 8   Develop a plan for the day.

ps 9   Set some short-term and long-term goals so as to have some direction in your life.

ps 10 Talk to God in prayer about your wounded self-esteem and pray for healing.

For Reflection, Journaling, or Discussion

1) On a scale of one to ten, with one being the lowest and ten being the highest, what number best describes your self-esteem today? Explain. _____

_____

_____

_____

_____

_____

_____

2) List five payoffs you could receive fairly soon (say in six months) for working on improving your self-esteem. _____

_____

_____

_____

_____

_____

_____

3) Identify three people in your life whose self-esteem you could give a little boost by your words and/or actions.

Name: _____ *What I could do or say:* _____

_____

_____

Name: _____ *What I could do or say:* _____

_____

_____

Name: _____ *What I could do or say:* _____

_____

_____

CHAPTER EIGHT

▲ ▽ ▲ ▽ ▲ ▽ ▲ ▽ ▲ ▽ ▲ ▽ ▲ ▽ ▲ ▽ ▲ ▽ ▲ ▽ ▲ ▽ ▲ ▽ ▲

Shame and Guilt: I Feel Badly about Who I Am and the Things I Have Done

INTRODUCTION

We all came into this world as innocent, unmarked babies who knew nothing about ourselves or our world, but we quickly learned that some of life is very good and some of life is quite painful. Most of us have had a lot of good <u>and</u> not-so-good experiences in life. We have enjoyed happy times and suffered through painful times. For some of us, life has been more painful than joyful. For others of us, life has been just the opposite—more joyful than painful. We have heard that we are created in God's image, that we are good, and that we are loved. Yet, we often have a hard time *believing* this. We may ask ourselves, "How can *I* be good? What about all the *bad* things I do? Doesn't that prove I am *not* good?!" Some of us may also ask, "Why do I feel so guilty? Why do I feel so bad about myself? What's wrong with me?"

In the last chapter, we identified factors such as parents, peers, success and failure, self-talk, and the media as having a significant impact upon your self-esteem. In this chapter we will explore two more factors that greatly influence how we feel about ourselves: shame and guilt. First we need to learn what shame and guilt are and how they differ from each other; then we will explore some practice skills to help us work through and beyond these feelings. As we work through our shame and guilt, *we will experience the joy of seeing and believing that we are indeed good people made in the image of our Creator.*

Without consulting a dictionary, define shame and guilt in your own words on the lines below:

Shame is _____

Guilt is _____

THE SHAM OF SHAME

Someone who is a sham is a fraud, a fake, a pretender. He or she is not what they pretend to be. Shame is a sham in that it tells us things that are <u>not</u> true about ourselves. Shame is often a liar! How does shame lie to us? Shame often tells us one or more of the following messages:

- You are a bad person.
- There is something wrong with you; you are a defective human being.
- There is something about you deep inside that is inadequate.
- You are worthless, no good, forever broken.
- You are not only *not* good, you are *damaged goods* and are incapable of being or doing good.

Wow! These are obviously very destructive and powerful messages if we believe them. Because shame tends to lie to us, we need to stand up and challenge these lies. If someone accused you of stealing a shirt from a store and you didn't do it, you would protest your innocence. It is not very likely that you would just let them cart you off to jail without trying to convince the authorities that you didn't do it. So it is with shame. When it attacks us with its lies, we need to resist it, challenge it, and fight back. We will learn some ways to do this later in the chapter.

Shame finds fault with our <u>personhood</u>—not our behavior. The "am" in "sh<u>am</u>e" is a good reminder that shame tries to tell me how I <u>am</u> as a person. And what it tends to tell you and me is destructive and untrue (see shame's messages above). Guilt, on the other hand, as we will see, tries to tell us about our poor behavior and is usually very truthful.

If you feel that you are a bad person or that something is wrong with you or that you are somehow different from others in a terrible way, you may be suffering from shame. Shame is an extremely powerful crippler of self-esteem and a robber of happiness. Fortunately, there are tools for fighting shame, which we will describe after we learn about guilt.

GUILT: FRIEND OR FOE? HEALTHY OR UNHEALTHY?

If sh<u>am</u>e tries to convince me that I <u>am</u> bad or that something is wrong with me, what is guilt? Guilt is about our <u>behavior</u>, what we have said or done, rather than about our personhood. Even though you and I are made in the image of God, we are also imperfect people who sometimes make poor choices. We *can* and *do* hurt others—and ourselves—by our words and actions. Guilt arises within us to tell us that we have hurt someone. We *need* its message, although it is painful, so that we can take some corrective action. We can always correct our behavior. We can't undo what we have done—there's a saying that even God cannot change the past—but we <u>can</u> often *correct* what we have done and/or try to do it better in the future. <u>Healthy guilt calls us to ACTION</u>:

<u>A</u>ctivate <u>C</u>aring <u>T</u>houghtful <u>I</u>ntelligent <u>O</u>ptions <u>N</u>ow !!!!

Guilt comes and visits us through our conscience. Guilt hurts very much when it arises with its message, but we are truly blessed if guilt causes us pain, because then we know we have a conscience that works very well. Guilt, when it calls our attention to something we have done to harm someone, is indeed a **friend**. True friends don't ignore our poor behavior; instead, they bring it to our attention in a respectful way so that we can be made aware of it and change it. The "ui" in the word "g<u>ui</u>lt" is a reminder that you (u) have been hurt or harmed in some way by what I (i) have done, by my *behavior*.

While overcoming shame can be, for some of us, a long battle against a very formidable foe, guilt can be dealt with much more quickly. We can be set free from guilt by simply apologizing for our harmful words or actions, making amends or restitution, and trying to do better next time. Guilt is one of the comparatively easier and quicker unpleasant emotions to work through. It still can be hard, though. It takes a mature and brave person to apologize to another. It takes a person with relatively healthy self-esteem to make amends to a person who has been hurt. We will identify a few practice skills to help us respond to our honest and much-needed friend, guilt.

Sometimes any emotion, whether pleasant or unpleasant, can get out of control. Guilt is one emotion that needs to be reined in when it wants to run wild. Left unchecked, guilt might tell us we are responsible for things that are way beyond our control and for which we are not responsible. For example, guilt-run-wild, **unhealthy guilt**, might tell us we are responsible for and should feel *bad* about the homeless and hungry, and therefore we have no right to enjoy food and shelter and other good things in life when so many are going without. While Christians are called to respond to social injustice and poverty, we should respond out of a desire to help others and share from our abundance because there is enough for everyone. We should help out of a sense of compassion and love—NOT GUILT. So when you and I respond to the poor and needy and hurting people in our world, we can ask ourselves, "Am I responding out of love and concern and compassion or because I feel guilty?"

What are some common behaviors of teens that result in a healthy sense of guilt? _____

_____

_____

_____

What are some things teens might feel guilty about for which they are not responsible? _____

_____

_____

_____

Guilt only becomes an enemy if it runs wild in our lives. Most of the time it can be a very helpful friend. Because guilt is a relatively easy, albeit painful, emotion to handle, let's look at some practice skills for coping with this emotion first. Then, we will explore some skills with which to fight the deeper and more powerful feeling of shame.

SIX PRACTICE SKILLS FOR DEALING WITH OUR FRIEND, HEALTHY GUILT

Practice Skill #1 First of all, when we are feeling guilty about something we have said or done, we need to face our guilt under the umbrella of God's love. Because guilt is painful and we can feel quite bad about our words or actions, we need to look at our behavior *with the support of God's love*. Earlier we mentioned that the "ui" in the word "guilt" stands for you (u) have been hurt by something I (i) did. The other letters in "guilt" also stand for truths we need to be aware of: the "g" stands for God, the "l" stands for love, and the "t" stands for together.

GUILT. Together with and under God's Love I look at my behavior that hurt yoU.

When we face our guilty feelings with the support of God's love, we are better able to see it in behavioral terms (I chose poorly) rather than in personhood terms (I am bad). God's love is our umbrella, which protects us from any shame-stones that might want to fall on us. This powerful love will support us when we feel badly about our behavior.

Practice Skill #2 Identify as specifically as possible what your harmful behavior was and what you would like to have done instead and admit this to yourself. Admitting we have done something wrong <u>to ourselves</u> is the first step toward healing. We can then go on to admitting our failure to God and to the person we have harmed. Did we say something hurtful? Did we fail to follow through on a commitment we had made to someone? Have we neglected an important relationship? We try to get very specific with what our behavior was. For example, we can feel bad about swearing at someone and wish we had used better language.

Practice Skill #3 Spend some time with God in prayer. We need to spend time with God because we are feeling the <u>necessary pain</u> that our healthy guilt has awakened in us. God wants to take our pain.

- **3a)** We can admit our fault, our poor or sinful behavior, to God and express sorrow for it.
   "Lord, I'm sorry I swore at Crystal. I wish I hadn't. . . . "
- **3b)** We can ask God for the courage and strength to apologize to the other person.
- **3c)** We can ask for the strength to *not* give up on ourselves and to try again. Maybe we have been working on reducing or eliminating our swearing. We may have had a temporary setback, which needn't stop us from trying again to use better language.
- **3d)** We can pray for the other person. Maybe we don't like this person. If so, we can ask God to help us see their good points or to be respectful of them, whether or not we will ever be friends.
- **3e)** We can pray to see the good in ourselves. Even though we chose poorly, *we are still good*. In the midst of our guilt, we may become temporarily blind to our self-goodness.

Practice Skill #4 **Talk to another person about what you have done wrong.** In the Bible we are encouraged to confess our sins: "*So then, confess your sins to one another and pray for one another, so that you will be healed.*" (Jas 5:16) Just admitting our fault to another person can be *so* helpful. Shame would want us to hide, and if we hide, our guilt grows in the dark. When we bring it out into the open, our guilt shrinks in the light. If you are Catholic, you have the sacrament of reconciliation, which is there to help you bring your sinful and poor choices into the light of God's love through another person, the priest. If you are Protestant, you may want to talk to a minister or someone else whom you can trust, and come to experience God's love by sharing the guilt you are feeling with him or her. We all, at times, need "God with some skin on." Another person can help us know God's forgiveness.

Practice Skill #5 **Admit your behavior to the other person, apologize for it, and be willing to make amends.** The previous practice skills prepare us for the most important and *risky* step: talking directly to the person we have harmed. Sometimes I want to just pray my guilt and ask God for forgiveness rather than face the person and ask for his or her forgiveness. But my guilt will not leave me alone until I apologize and make amends to the person I have hurt. It is risky to apologize because the other person might still be angry with us—and might tell us how angry they are! Or they may reject our apology! Or they may say our apology won't undo the harm we have done! In most cases, however, people will accept our apology and our offer to make amends—to make it right. If they reject our apology, we may need to give them more time. We could choose to write them a letter a week or two later. Perhaps by then their anger will have softened. . . . If they still reject our apology and desire to make amends, we need to let it go. We have done all *we* could to restore the relationship. We can't control how the *other person* will respond to us nor can we force them to respond in the way we would like.

5a) When we apologize we want to *specifically* name our behavior and state our remorse for it. We would not say to Crystal "I'm sorry if I have ever done anything to hurt you." That's not being direct and specific. Instead, we would say, "I am sorry for swearing at you the other day. I really regret doing that. I'm trying hard not to swear at all. I hope you can forgive me."

5b) After we apologize, we *stop talking* and allow the other person time to respond to us. We might be so afraid of their response that we fill the silence with constant chatter. "I hope you can forgive me, but if you can't, I understand. I really didn't mean to swear at you. I hope you can forgive me. . . . " By then, they may have something else to get mad at us about: our incessant talking!! We are called to apologize, not grovel in the dirt, which we do when looking for worms!

5c) Sometimes an apology isn't good enough. We need to try to correct our poor choice, fix it. If we have broken something of someone's or taken something, we would want to pay for it or return it. Imagine how we would feel if someone said to us, "I'm sorry I took your bike, but I'm *not* going to return it." How sorry can they be?! Sometimes we *can't* "fix it," so we look for some other way to show we care. For example, with Crystal, we can't take back the swear words we have spoken, but we *can* choose to be more complimentary of her or go out of our way to help her when we see an opportunity to do so.

Practice Skill #6 **Forgive ourselves.** Regardless of *how* the other person responded to our apology—even if they rejected our apology—we need to forgive ourselves. We can have the other person forgive us, have God forgive us, but if we don't forgive ourselves, we are still in guilt's vise. You might choose to say forgiving words to yourself aloud in the privacy of your bedroom. "I forgive myself completely for swearing at Crystal. I know God still loves me and I choose to love myself right now."

Do you have a hard time forgiving yourself for the mistakes and poor choices you make? Explain.

_____

_____

_____

FIVE PRACTICE SKILLS FOR WAGING WAR UPON AND OVERCOMING SHAME

A deep sense of shame, of defectiveness, or of being fundamentally flawed in some way requires the care of professionals. Because shame impacts and affects so many aspects of our lives—our relationships with ourselves, other people, and God; our ability or inability to have success at school; our energy level—it requires the care and treatment of the helping professions. Not only are supportive people needed when we are sunk in shame, but <u>highly competent</u> professional counselors and/or clergy are needed as well.

We can think of shame in terms of disease. If we had cancer, we would definitely want emotionally supportive family and friends to be at our side, <u>BUT</u> we would most benefit from their support if we also went to a doctor and got the professional medical help we needed. The support from our family and friends would <u>not</u> be an effective substitute for receiving medical care. Shame is like a cancer within us that negatively impacts many areas of our lives—including our ability to be happy. Jesus wants us to have life, and life to the full! Shame is a happiness robber. What follows are a few practice skills that can be helpful for many of us as we work toward discovering our own foundational and fundamental God-given goodness.

<u>Practice Skill #1</u> **Try some or all of the practice skills mentioned in the previous chapter on self-esteem (see pp. 64–68).** Since shame so negatively affects our self-esteem, the self-esteem practice skills can be helpful to us: keeping a record of what we do well each day; practicing affirmations; surrounding ourselves with healthy and supportive people; avoiding comparisons that always have us on the bottom looking up; asking for the help of others to see our own goodness; choosing an area for self-improvement; using "I choose" statements; making some daily plans; setting short- and long-term goals; and bringing our shame before our tender and compassionate God for healing.

<u>Practice Skill #2</u> **Plan a ceremony or ritual or party to celebrate <u>YOU</u>!** Because shame leads us to feeling *so* bad about ourselves, having a party or celebration for ourselves is an insult to shame and a huge step of liberation for us! We don't need to feel *totally* wonderful about ourselves in order to have a party; in fact, we can feel quite rotten. By having a **self-celebration** we are taking a positive and

powerful step to fight shame head-on. Our efforts, along with the healing we experience through others, plus God's love and support are <u>way more powerful</u> than shame!! Having a party is honoring the "our efforts" part of the formula for healing. We will have a sense of personal power as we gather a few people together in OUR name! <u>Shame</u> will try to convince us we are not worthy of this special attention, but it is <u>not</u> in charge of our lives any longer—<u>WE ARE!</u>

<u>Practice Skill #3</u> **Make a list of your good qualities and the good things you have done in your life— no matter how small—and post it in your bedroom where you will see it every day.** Maybe your first reaction is, "There won't be anything on my list!" If so, and I felt this way about myself at one point in my life, we ask for the help of others to see and name our goodness. Again, shame *wants* us to feel bad and think we *are* bad in some way. Naming and posting and reading and rereading our goodness is a direct attack on shame! This is a war of sorts we are engaged in. We don't want to sit in a hole and let shame "bomb" us with its endless negative lies about and to us. Instead, we get out of our hole, counterattack, and <u>stick up for ourselves!!</u> That's a big learning for us shame-bound people: we are worthy of standing up for and protecting ourselves! WE NEED TO LEARN HOW TO FIGHT!

Whether you are wrestling with shame or not, make a long list of all that is good about you:

_____

_____

_____

_____

_____

_____

<u>Practice Skill #4</u> **Make a list of Bible verses that speak of your worth and value in the eyes of the most powerful and loving and tender force in the universe: GOD.** You may ask a friend or parent or pastor or priest to help you locate some of these verses. You might also refer to the indexes in the back of most Bibles and/or the appendix in the back of this book as an aid to discovering these healing words of God. You might want to be creative in how you write them down. Here are a few suggestions:

- Perhaps you could buy a special journal and write these verses with colored pencils.
- Write a verse on a piece of paper and carry it in your pocket and read it a few times each day when no one is looking.
- Copy a verse and put the piece of paper under your pillow at night as a way of letting God love you while you sleep.
- Read one or more of these verses aloud three times every day so that you also *hear* these words being spoken to you.
- Tape one or more of these verses under a favorite picture of Jesus and as you look at the picture, imagine the words being spoken to <u>you</u>.
- Commit a couple of verses to memory so that when shame wants to lie to you about your defectiveness, you can counter with the <u>truth of your value and importance in God's eyes!</u>

• Substitute your name in these verses wherever it says "Jerusalem" or some other biblical name, so that it will be easier to know they are meant for you. (See the sample verse below.)

Isaiah 49:15–16 . . . *I will never forget you. Jerusalem (write your own name in place of Jerusalem),* _____ *, I can never forget you! I have written your name on the palms of my hands!*

Practice Skill #5 **Practice self-kindness and self-gentleness every day.** If some days we forget to be kind or gentle with ourselves, we try again the next day. We can keep an image of a baby or small child before us to help us be gentle with ourselves. Maybe we can look at a baby or childhood picture of ourselves to remind us. I use a picture of myself in first grade because I like that picture of me. We wouldn't be rough with a baby or child; because we were once innocent babies, too, we try to be gentle and tender with ourselves.

Ultimately, *we* have to decide to be good to *ourselves.* You are the one you are with all the time. You can practice being kind and gentle and good to yourself each day, and pretty soon this self-care will become a habit and the self-neglect and/or self-abuse that is often a part of a shame-driven person's repertoire will fade away. In its place will grow a new you who sees that *indeed you are* a good and valuable person worthy of self-respect and gentleness and kindness all the days of your life.

What specific things can you do to show gentleness and respect to yourself? _____

_____

_____

_____

CHAPTER RECAP

1) Shame is a powerful crippler of self-esteem for many of us.

2) Shame is a sham that tells the big lie that we are *bad* or in some way defective people.

3) The "am" in "sh<u>am</u>e" reminds us that shame attacks our personhood: "I AM bad. . . . "

4) The *Truth* that we are good and created good by God is more powerful than shame.

5) Guilt, on the other hand, is an honest friend that arises when we have done something wrong.

6) Guilt is about our behavior, what we have said or done, and not about our personhood.

7) Healthy guilt calls us to ACTION—to apologize and make amends when possible.

8) The "ui" in the word "g<u>ui</u>lt" tells me that yo**u** (u) have been hurt by something **I** (i) said or did.

9) Six practice skills (ps) for resolving guilt are to:

ps 1 Face our guilt under the umbrella of God's love so that God can support us.
ps 2 Specifically identify what our hurtful behavior was and admit this to ourselves.
ps 3 Spend some time in prayer for forgiveness and for the courage to apologize to the person.
ps 4 Talk to another person about what we have done wrong. Confessing to another is helpful.
ps 5 Admit our behavior to the person we have hurt, apologize for it, and be willing to make amends.
ps 6 Forgive ourselves. God forgives us and usually the person we hurt will forgive us. Will we forgive ourselves?

10) Five practice skills (ps) for waging war upon and overcoming **shame** are:

ps 1 Try some or all of the practice skills mentioned in the self-esteem chapter.
ps 2 Plan a ceremony or ritual or party to celebrate YOU!
ps 3 Make a list of your good qualities and the good things you have done, post it, and read it.
ps 4 Make a list of Bible verses that speak of your worth and value in God's eyes.
ps 5 Practice self-kindness and self-gentleness every day.

For Reflection, Journaling, or Discussion

*1) What information from this chapter might be helpful for the times when you feel guilt?*_____
_____
_____

2) Try to see yourself as God sees you and name the goodness that is in you: _____
_____
_____

3) If you were Eric in the following situation, how would you go about resolving your feelings of shame and guilt?

Eric had another huge fight with his parents last night. In the midst of the argument, Eric screamed and swore at his parents and told them he never wanted to see them again as he stormed out of the house. Today he is feeling a lot of guilt for what he said and feels like he is a "bad" person.

If I were Eric I would

_____
_____
_____
_____

CHAPTER NINE

▲ ▽ ▲ ▽ ▲ ▽ ▲ ▽ ▲ ▽ ▲ ▽ ▲ ▽ ▲ ▽ ▲ ▽ ▲ ▽ ▲ ▽ ▲ ▽ ▲ ▽ ▲

Loneliness, Sadness, and Rejection: They All HURT!

INTRODUCTION

Imagine yourself home on a Saturday with nothing to do. You had made plans to go the mall with some friends but discovered they left without you! The chances are you would be feeling very lonely, sad, and rejected. You might ask yourself, "Why did they go without me? I don't understand—don't they like me anymore?"

To be home when others are out having fun is the pits for most teens. Sadness grows more powerful as each minute drags on. Your sense of being rejected hurts deeply. Your parents might try to cheer you up, but you seem unable to shake that feeling of loneliness. So-called helpful suggestions from your mom or dad prove to be anything *but* helpful. They just don't understand how doing something with *them* is <u>not</u> the same as doing something with your friends!

Experiencing loneliness, sadness, and rejection are an unpleasant and painful part of life. Everyone has felt the misery of these feelings from time to time. They are very difficult emotions, not only for teens, but for adults as well. One reason they are so difficult, besides the pain they can cause, is that we sometimes think we should *never* feel lonely, sad, or rejected. We can be surprised when these feelings swell up within us, and they might catch us off guard and overpower us. We may find ourselves sinking quickly like a torpedoed ship and feel powerless to save ourselves. But these feelings <u>will</u> move on—*especially* if we allow ourselves to feel them and take some steps to help ourselves. There is a lifeboat we can climb into which will bring us safely to shore. To think that we should never feel lonely or sad or rejected is as unrealistic as thinking we should never feel the joy of companionship, happiness, and acceptance!

How do you handle your feelings of sadness, loneliness, and/or rejection? _____

_____

Sometimes to find a great treasure a person has to dig and go beneath the surface. So it is with these three painful and difficult emotions. We need to dig a little deeper to discover the truth about them so that they don't overwhelm and overpower us as much.

In this chapter we will uncover some untruths and faulty beliefs we might have about these emotions and dig for deeper truths that can, hopefully, set us free from their painful grip. We will first dig out the untruths about these feelings, lay a foundation of new truths, and then build some practice skills for dealing with them.

THREE UNTRUTHS AND NEW TRUTHS
ABOUT LONELINESS

1) Untruth: You will <u>never</u> feel lonely if you have enough friends, are more popular, or have a special relationship with a boyfriend or girlfriend.

New Truth: Loneliness is a feeling you will experience on a regular basis throughout your life—even if you are popular and have lots of friends. When you are older and have a special relationship with someone, you will *still* feel lonely at times.

2) Untruth: Loneliness means that something is wrong with you and that you are unloved by people and perhaps even by God!

New Truth: The fact that you sometimes feel lonely means that you are a perfectly normal human being. The "one" in the word "loneliness" is a reminder that each of us is an individual who comes into this world alone and who goes out of this world alone on his or her journey to being with God forever. We truly *need* the love and support of others in this life, but each of us, although very much connected to and dependent upon family, friends, and many other people, is still a separate, unique individual. God, however, is *never* separated from us and, in fact, dwells *within* us! So, although you and I are separate from everyone else in the world in some ways, we are *always* connected to God— even though we don't always *feel* this connectedness.

3) Untruth: Loneliness just comes and goes and has no other purpose than to tell us we are lonely for people.

New Truth: While loneliness does come and go, it can tell us that we are *not* only lonely for other people, but also lonely for *God* or lonely for *ourselves.*

a) **People loneliness.** Loneliness may tell us we need to take some <u>action</u> to connect with others. We can't always sit by the phone and hope someone will call *us* when we are feeling lonely. If our phone is not ringing, we can pick it up and make someone else's phone ring!

b) **God loneliness.** It may tell us we need to spend some time with God, because there is a loneliness that arises from our need for God and that *only* God can fill. We can lessen this loneliness for God by spending some time with God in prayer. Other people in our lives cannot fill our "God-loneliness," just as God cannot fill our "people-loneliness." I wonder if God ever feels lonely for us.

c) **Self-loneliness.** We may become lonely for ourselves at times, as strange as that may sound. Jesus tells us to love our neighbor as we love *ourselves*. One way to love ourselves is to spend some time with and by ourselves. Oftentimes a little quiet and alone time to relax and sort things out can be as refreshing as spending time with God and others. Neither people nor God can meet this need to be a friend to ourselves.

Does it make sense that we can feel lonely for God or ourselves? Why or why not? _____

_____

_____

_____

FOUR UNTRUTHS AND NEW TRUTHS ABOUT SADNESS

1) Untruth: It is possible to *never* feel sadness and *always* feel happy.

New Truth: As we mentioned before, constant happiness is <u>not</u> a realistic goal; it is a fantasy. Sadness is part of life. When we say something like, "I hope you'll always be happy," it is a wish for happiness and joy for the other person. We truly want the recipient of this message to have a good and satisfying life, but we don't expect that he or she will *never* feel unhappy.

2) Untruth: Sadness is an emotion we should try to avoid feeling as much as possible because other people don't like to be around someone who is sad.

New Truth: Sadness, like every other unpleasant feeling, is one we need to face and deal with. True friends, who really care about us, can accept that we will feel sad at times and not abandon us in our sad moments.

3) Untruth: When someone is sad it is *our* responsibility to cheer them up.

New Truth: Each person is always responsible for feeling and dealing with her or her own emotions, including sadness. Likewise, you and I are responsible for our own feelings, including the times *we* feel sad. Sometimes when we are sad, the last thing we want or need is someone trying to cheer us up! It can be more helpful and healing if we just stay with our sad feelings for a while and *feel* them rather than try to instantly get rid of them (which we can't do anyway). Oftentimes we would be helped more by having someone listen to us, and when we receive this gift of attentive listening, our sadness will frequently decrease in its intensity. The old saying, "Sorrows shared are divided," is very true when friends and family offer their support to each other in times of sadness.

Tell about a time when the support of a friend or family member helped you through your sadness.

_____

_____

_____

4) Untruth: Sadness has no purpose other than to tell us we are feeling sad.

New Truth: Sadness, like all the unpleasant and painful emotions, has a reason for arising within us and a message for us. It frequently tells us that something is missing in our lives. The "ad" in the word "sad" is a reminder that we need to add something to our lives, such as a friend, or some time with God, or some goals and direction in life. . . . Sadness can also tell us that something we once had is no longer there: a pet, an old neighborhood, a friend who moved away, a loved one who died. . . .

TWO UNTRUTHS AND NEW TRUTHS ABOUT REJECTION

1) Untruth: Being rejected is *always* bad.

New Truth: Rejection, although *always* painful, can be a blessing at times. Sometimes when we are rejected by a group of people or by a certain person, it turns out to be good because someone who is better for us is going to come into our lives. Without first being rejected, we might miss this opportunity for a better situation or a more compatible person to come into our lives. The "ejection" in "rejection" reminds us that we don't always leave willingly; sometimes we have to be forced out, ejected!

For example, if some of your friends start using drugs and reject you because you choose not to use, then this rejection is really a great blessing. You might have to go through the pain of losing some of your friends, but you will make new ones who are making healthier choices. The rejection (ejection) by your old friends cleared the way for better and healthier relationships to develop. In this case, rejection turned out to be better than acceptance!

Another example might be not making a particular team that you tried out for. Your rejection from, say, the basketball team might lead you to discover and enjoy another sport that you are better at, such as volleyball or soccer!

What are two more examples of how being rejected could actually turn out to be a blessing?

1) _____

2) _____

2) Untruth: If the people with whom we either want to have a friendship or already do have a friendship are *healthy* and end up rejecting us, something is wrong with us.

New Truth: There's an old saying that states the only thing that stays the same in life is *change*. The fact is people change and relationships change. A friend, with whom you once shared many interests, may develop a new interest that does not appeal to you. The fact that your friend wants to spend time on his or her new interest is not a sign that anything is wrong with you *or* your friend. What is likely to happen is you will no longer spend as much time together. And it may take awhile to develop a new friendship that can fill the void left by your old friend. It may feel like rejection, and you will almost certainly feel sadness, but what has really happened is that you have each grown in different ways. Your challenge is to <u>not</u> take it personally. There are very few people we walk with in life from our birth to our grave. Usually what happens is we have companions for a certain part of our life journey and discover new companions for a different part of our journey and so on.

Who are some friends you enjoyed spending time with when you were younger and don't see anymore? _____

_____

_____

REJECTION: A TRUE STORY WITH A HAPPY ENDING

As an adult, I was rejected by two different women with whom I had relationships at different times. I cared very much for each of them, so when I was rejected, it *really* hurt. Looking back on the situations, I realized that we just grew in different directions. If I hadn't been <u>rejected</u>, I might never have met the woman I eventually married and who became the mother of my children! At the time I was rejected, *ejected*, all I could feel was pain. But eventually the pain subsided and I was able to pursue other interests and friendships. You, too, are going to have close relationships that will end. It is very unlikely the girlfriend or boyfriend that you might have in high school or college will end up being the person you marry. Just remember that you <u>can</u> survive the times when relationships change or end.

SEVEN PRACTICE SKILLS FOR DEALING WITH LONELINESS, SADNESS, AND REJECTION

Now that we have dug up some of the untruths about these three feelings and have laid a foundation of new truths, let's look at some practice skills that can help us deal with these emotions. In a previous chapter we learned that feelings sometimes come along in twos and threes rather than one by one. For instance, we can feel peace and joy at the same time or anger and hate at the same time.

The three emotions we are examining in this chapter frequently appear in twos and threes. Oftentimes a practice skill for handling one of these emotions can also be used in coping with the other two. So, what follows is *one* list of skills from which you can choose to deal with your feelings of loneliness, sadness, and/or rejection. These skills will <u>not</u> automatically take away your pain, but sometimes they can help *lessen the intensity* of these unpleasant feelings.

<u>Practice Skill #1</u> **Try to name as precisely as possible what you are feeling and why you are feeling it.** Our unpleasant feelings can be so painful at times that we don't know *what* we are feeling. One thing we *do* know for sure is that <u>we are in pain and it hurts!</u> A challenge for us is to try to name what we are feeling and why. If we can't figure out the why, we can at least regain some control of ourselves by naming what we are feeling. By *naming* we are *taming* the wildness of the emotion. Maybe all we can say is, "Right now I feel very sad and I don't know why." Other times we might be able to clearly identify the reason for our sadness: someone just rejected us.

<u>Practice Skill #2</u> **Develop relationships with and call upon supportive friends and family to help you through these painful feelings.** There's hardly anything worse than feeling sad or lonely or rejected and having no one to turn to! That's why it is *so* important to work on developing and sustaining healthy friendships and relationships. When you are lonely or sad, you then have some people to call upon and lean on. Your friends can also lean on you when they are suffering rejection or loneliness or sadness. Sometimes teens make the mistake of getting too involved with one person of the opposite sex. They neglect their family and friendships, and when the relationship with this special person changes or ends, they have no one to turn to. A well-balanced teen has a variety of relationships with members of both sexes.

Who are you most likely to turn to when feeling lonely or sad or rejected? _____

_____

<u>Practice Skill #3</u> **Implode.** To implode means to burst inward. It is the opposite of explode, which we do outwardly sometimes when we feel angry or rageful. Rather than try to hold these feelings deep inside us, we allow them to burst. With this practice skill we really *get into* the feeling and feel it with all its power. We *need* to feel it and can't bat it away any more than we can get over our feelings of hate without first feeling hatred. So we allow ourselves to feel the pain of these feelings and cry and feel sorry for ourselves. Jesus had pity for people who were hurting when he walked the earth. We, made in the image of God, can have pity for ourselves. The chances are if we allow ourselves to really *feel* these feelings, even though it is absolutely no fun, they will move out of us. Many times a good cry—even for young men—can cleanse a hurting heart as well as a shower can cleanse the body.

<u>Practice Skill #4</u> **Avoid extreme thinking and strive for reasonable thinking.** Extreme thinking goes like this: "<u>No one</u> likes me." "<u>Everyone</u> hates me." "I will <u>never</u> have friends." "I will <u>always</u> feel sad." Some big clues that we are engaging in extreme thinking is when we are having negative thoughts that include words such as <u>NO ONE</u>, <u>EVERYONE</u>, <u>NEVER</u>, and <u>ALWAYS</u>. These statements are untrue and can only become true if we *choose* to behave in such a way that makes them become a reality. If I never let people like me, then it may turn out to be true that no one *does* like me. But I have to put a lot of effort into making that negative belief become a reality. It takes much less work to have a least one person like me in this world! So we work on identifying our extreme thoughts and

changing them to more reasonable thoughts. If we stay stuck in extreme thinking, we suffer much more from these feelings than if we redirect our thinking.

Here are three examples of a teen exchanging extreme thinking for more reasonable thinking:

Extreme thinking	Reasonable thinking
• No one likes me.	This is not true. Sarah likes me, so does Randy and . . .
• I am no good!	There's lots that's good about me, for instance . . .
• I will never be happy!	I was happy last Friday at the dance. I will be happy again.

Add two more

Extreme thinking	**Reasonable thinking**
1)_____	_____
_____	_____
2)_____	_____
_____	_____

<u>Practice Skill #5</u> **Look back on your life for evidence of how you have survived these painful feelings before.** Sometimes when young people feel sad or lonely or rejected, they think these feelings will <u>never</u> end. The pain can be very excruciating, and when you are in a lot of emotional pain, your thinking becomes unclear. This is when our memory can be a big help to us. We look back and remember other times of sadness or loneliness or rejection, which no longer cause us pain, as evidence that these <u>current painful feelings will pass!</u> We have survived these feelings before, so we will again! Our own history proves this!

<u>Practice Skill #6</u> **Because the "ad" in "sad" tells you that something is missing in your life, you can try to determine what this missing element might be and develop a plan for how to fill this need.** Maybe you are in need of a friend. How can you increase your chances of developing friendships? Maybe a loved one has died. You cannot bring this person back to life, but you can grieve his or her absence and eventually recall the meaningful times you had with each other. Perhaps you could choose to write a letter to your loved one saying how much he or she is missed.

Identifying our need does <u>not</u> immediately satisfy the longing, but it brings to our awareness what we are missing and sad about. Once we are aware, we can begin to take some concrete steps to "add" to our lives what is missing, when possible.

<u>Practice Skill #7</u> **Choose constructive rather than destructive actions. Remind yourself that this feeling <u>will</u> pass!** Pain can overwhelm people of all ages, and sometimes suicidal or other destructive thoughts come into a person's mind. It is <u>so</u> important to NOT DO ANYTHING TO HARM YOURSELF! THESE PAINFUL FEELINGS WILL MOVE ON EVENTUALLY! If you are considering hurting yourself, call 911. The operator can put you in contact with someone who will be able to understand the pain you are experiencing and help you through it. You might also refer to one of the phone numbers in appendix 1 of this book as a place to go for help. Or perhaps a counselor at a school, a teacher, or a pastor can help you through your pain. <u>There are many caring people who</u>

are willing to help you! A wise and mature young person is not afraid to ask for help when he or she needs it. Throughout this book, we have identified many practice skills to help us with our painful feelings. Hopefully, one or more of these skills can help you help yourself through this painful time.

Make a list of eight healthy and constructive choices you can choose from when you are feeling very sad and down:

1) _____   5) _____

2) _____   6) _____

3) _____   7) _____

4) _____   8) _____

CHAPTER RECAP

1) Feeling sad, lonely, and/or rejected is no fun, yet we will experience these feeling regularly throughout life.

2) We need to uncover untruths and faulty beliefs we may have about these three emotions and replace them with new truths.

- Untruths about loneliness: You will never feel lonely if you have enough friends, are more popular, or have a special relationship; feeling lonely means that something is wrong with you or that you are unloved; the only purpose of loneliness is to tell you that you need people.
- New truths about loneliness: Feelings of loneliness will come and go no matter how many friends we have; even when we have a lot of love in our lives, we will still feel lonely because we are separate from each other in some ways; we can be lonely for people but also for God and for ourselves.
- Untruths about sadness: It is possible to *always* be happy and never sad; we should try to avoid sadness because people don't like to be around us when we are sad; it is our responsibility to cheer up those who are sad; the only purpose of sadness is to tell us we are sad.
- New truths about sadness: Constant happiness is not a realistic goal because sadness is part of life; true friends can accept us when we are sad and will not abandon us; the person who is sad is responsible for his or her own feelings; the "ad" in "sad" tells us that, when possible, we need to add something to our lives that is missing.
- Untruths about rejection: Being rejected is always bad; if the person who rejects us is healthy and still rejects us, something is wrong with us.
- New truths about rejection: Rejection, although always painful, can be a blessing; sometimes we experience rejection because people and relationships change.

3) Seven practice skills (ps) for coping with loneliness, sadness, and rejection are:

ps 1   Try to name as exactly as possible what you are feeling and why you are feeling it.

ps 2   Develop and call upon your supportive friends and family to help you through these painful feelings.

ps 3 Implode. Let the pain of these emotions burst within you rather than stuffing them.

ps 4 Avoid extreme thinking and strive for reasonable thinking.

ps 5 Look back on your life for evidence of how you have survived these painful feelings before.

ps 6 Because the "ad" in "sad" tells you that something is missing in your life, try to determine what this missing element might be and develop a plan for filling this need.

ps 7 Choose constructive rather than destructive actions. Remind yourself that this feeling will pass.

For Reflection, Journaling, or Discussion

1) What do you need in your life in order to be happier than you are? What steps can you take to enjoy greater happiness? Or if you are already pretty happy, tell why. _____

_____

_____

_____

_____

2) Describe some of the happiest moments of your life during the past year. What factors influenced this happy time in your life? _____

_____

_____

_____

*Describe some of the saddest moments of your life during the past year. What was happening in your life that left you feeling so sad?*_____

_____

_____

_____

_____

3) Ask your mom or dad how they experienced and handled rejection when they were your age.

_____

_____

_____

_____

Appendix 1

▲ ▼ ▲ ▼ ▲ ▼ ▲ ▼ ▲ ▼ ▲ ▼ ▲ ▼ ▲ ▼ ▲ ▼ ▲ ▼ ▲ ▼ ▲

People Who Can Help Me during a Tough and Painful Time

911   Emergency Operator

1-800-231-6946   National Runaway Hotline

1-800-HIT-HOME   Hit Home (counseling for teen alcohol and drug abuse)

Take a minute and look up the numbers below so that you can use them in time of need:

Ph: pastor or priest

Ph: doctor

Ph: school or family counselor

Ph: youth director

Ph: parent's work number

Ph: relative's phone number

Other emergency phone numbers from the front of your phone book that may be helpful:

Ph: Suicide Prevention: _____

Ph: Crisis Intervention: _____

Ph: Agency: _____

Ph: Agency: _____

Ph: Agency: _____

Three friends I can call in a time of need:

Ph: Name: _____

Ph: Name: _____

Ph: Name: _____

APPENDIX 2

▲ ▽ ▲ ▽ ▲ ▽ ▲ ▽ ▲ ▽ ▲ ▽ ▲ ▽ ▲ ▽ ▲ ▽ ▲ ▽ ▲ ▽ ▲

TWENTY TENDER VERSES FOR TOUGH TIMES

Isaiah 41:13	I am the Lord your God; I strengthen you and tell you, "Do not be afraid; I will help you."
James 4:8	Come near to God, and he will come near to you.
Psalm 59:10	My God loves me and will come to me. . . .
Psalm 42:11	Why am I so sad? Why am I so troubled? I will put my hope in God, my savior and my God.
Philippians 4:13	I have the strength to face all conditions by the power that Christ gives me.
Psalm 118:6	The Lord is with me, I will not be afraid; what can anyone do to me?
Philippians 4:6	Don't worry about anything, but in all your prayers ask God for what you need, always asking him with a thankful heart.
John 1:5	The light shines in the darkness, and the darkness has never put it out.
Matthew 11:28	Come to me, all of you who are tired of carrying heavy loads, and I will give you rest.
Ephesians 2:4	God's mercy is so abundant, and his love for us is so great.
Philippians 2:1	Your life in Christ makes you strong, and his love comforts you.
Matthew 28:20	I will be with you always. . . .
Mark 10:14	Let the children come to me, and do not stop them, because the kingdom of God belongs to such as these.
Psalm 103:12	As far as the east is from the west, so far does he remove our sin from us.
John 8:11	Jesus said, "I do not condemn you. . . . "
James 2:13	Mercy triumphs over judgment.
Luke 1:78	Our God is merciful and tender.
John 14:27	Peace is what I leave with you; it is my own peace I give you. I do not give it as the world does. Do not be worried and upset; do not be afraid.
Jeremiah 29:11	I alone know the plans I have for you, plans to bring you prosperity and not disaster, plans to bring about the future you hope for.
Psalm 40:11	Lord, I know you will never stop being merciful to me. Your love and loyalty will always keep me safe.